BASIC SKILLS

For Academic Reading

DATE DUE			
NO 30 98			
MR 1 6 99			
MY 1 0 00			
JE 15 01			
NO 8 01			
NO 15 00			
AP 1 9 10			
MY 1 0 10			

DEMCO 38-296

BASIC SKILLS
For Academic Reading

JAMES W. RAMSAY

Illustrations by

Paul Martin

PRENTICE HALL REGENTS, Englewood Cliffs, New Jersey 07632

Editorial/production supervision and
    interior design: Patricia V. Amoroso
Cover design: Ben Santora
Manufacturing buyer: Harry P. Baisley

©1986 by Prentice Hall Regents
Prentice-Hall, Inc.
A Simon & Schuster Company
Englewood Cliffs, New Jersey 07632

Printed in the United States of America

15   14   13   12

ISBN 0-13-066036-1   01

PRENTICE-HALL INTERNATIONAL (UK) LIMITED, *London*
PRENTICE-HALL OF AUSTRALIA PTY. LIMITED, *Sydney*
PRENTICE-HALL OF CANADA INC., *Toronto*
PRENTICE-HALL HISPANOAMERICANA, S. A., *Mexico City*
PRENTICE-HALL OF INDIA PRIVATE LIMITED, *New Delhi*
PRENTICE-HALL OF JAPAN, INC., *Tokyo*
PRENTICE-HALL OF SOUTHEAST ASIA PTE. LTD., *Singapore*
EDITORA PRENTICE-HALL DO BRASIL, LTDA., *Rio de Janeiro*

To Celeste
for whom it was written

and Janet
who made it possible

Contents

Introduction

Basic Skills for Academic Reading is intended for adult learners of English as a second language who are preparing to attend universities or training programs in which they will need to read English for academic purposes. The text is intended for use at the beginning and intermediate levels of intensive English programs in the United States and abroad. The text may be used to introduce the basic skills of reading in English, or it may be used as a review of those skills. It is assumed that students who use this text will be high school graduates who have previously studied some English, for a knowledge of basic English vocabulary and the ability to read simple English sentences are required.

The book consists of alternating units of reading skills exercises and units of reading passages with comprehension exercises. This format makes it easier for the teacher (or the self-study learner) to pick and choose from the material in the skills units and the reading passage units, in order to select those materials most suited to individual and group needs. For example, the reading speed exercises will be particularly helpful for those learners whose native language alphabet is distinctly different from that of English, while some of these exercises might not be necessary for other learners. The text can be used slowly with beginning-level learners, as a rapid review for intermediate-level learners, or for independent study. It can be used intensively in programs that allot ample time for teaching reading, or selectively in programs with little time allotted to reading. A scope and sequence chart and vocabulary list have been provided to aid the classroom teacher.

Each reading skills unit is designed to introduce the necessary skills and vocabulary for the unit of reading passages that follows. In addition, each reading passage is preceded by a vocabulary preparation exercise and followed by comprehension exercises designed to assess literal and interpretive understanding of the passage.

Suggestions for Using the Reading Skills Exercises

Word Study These exercises are designed to encourage learners to discover the meanings of new vocabulary items by using the vocabulary acquisition skills they will need as readers of academic texts. Many of the new words that will appear in the reading passages are introduced in these exercises. While learners are doing these exercises, it is important that they rely on their own judgment and, where possible, consult with others in their class or group in order to develop independent vocabulary acquisition strategies.

Sentence Study These exercises require learners to distinguish between phrases and sentences that are synonymous, similar, or different in meaning. They are designed not only to improve comprehension through analysis of complex grammatical constructions at the sentence level, but also to help learners develop those "synthesis" skills necessary for bringing together information effectively in note-taking, paraphrasing, and summary-writing. These exercises are particularly effective when used with small groups in which each learner defends his or her judgment, and the group attempts to arrive at a consensus for the best answer, which can then be checked with the classroom teacher. The success of this approach depends on the group's willingness to determine *why* one answer is better than the others, instead of depending on the teacher as a source of correct answers.

Paragraph Study These exercises are designed to improve comprehension of connected discourse through analysis of paragraph structure and development as well as through "synthesis" of the essential information from a text in note, diagram, or outline form. Again, these exercises are particularly effective when used with small groups, as there is often more than one possible interpretation of the arrangement of information in a text. Learners should be encouraged to discuss any differences in interpretation in order to achieve greater understanding of the implications of a text.

Reading Speed These exercises progress from rapid recognition of the graphic representation of identical words and phrases to rapid mediation of the meanings of different words, phrases, and sentences. They are intended to prepare learners for reading through an entire text, rather than stopping at each unfamiliar word, in order to grasp the overall meaning of the text. Suggested reading times are given for each exercise, and an element of competition can be introduced by announcing the end of the suggested time and counting the number of students who were able to complete the exercise within that time. Checking of the exercises is best done in pairs; books are exchanged and any mistakes are pointed out by the partner.

Suggestions for Using the Reading Passages

Introduction and Questions for Discussion These are intended to interest the reader in the topic of the passage to be read so that appropriate hypotheses about the content of the passage can be formed, based on personal experience and knowledge of the topic. The introductions can be used as the focus of class or small group discussions of the learners' expectations about the passage, and the questions for discussion in Unit 8 can be used for an exchange of information between learners about the topic of the passage.

Vocabulary Preparation These exercises are designed to reinforce the vocabulary acquisition skills introduced in the reading skills units by helping the reader discover the meanings of vocabulary items to be encountered in the reading passage. If both the introduction and vocabulary preparation exercises are discussed before attempting the reading passage, the reader should be prepared to read the passage with fluency and minimal frustration.

Text and Comprehension Questions The reading passages are intended to be readable for beginning-level ESL learners, yet representative of the discourse and style of most academic writing. Much time is spent on preparing learners for reading each passage in order to enable them to read the passage quickly enough to grasp the overall meaning. The "Yes or No" and "True or False" comprehension questions are designed to be used as a quick check of overall comprehension after the first reading of the passage, so it is suggested that the learner be asked not to refer back to the text while answering these questions. The multiple choice and short answer questions, on the other hand, are more interpretive and learners will often find it necessary to refer to the text in order to answer these questions. The "What Do You Think?" questions are intended to encourage learners to think critically about what they have read and (where possible) to discuss their opinions with others.

Additional Readings One passage in each unit of reading passages includes additional readings, short passages on topics related to the topic of the text. These additional readings are designed to provide practice in reading without the preparation exercises that precede the other passages. They are also intended to provide practice in integrating information from different sources in order to arrive at a more complete understanding of a topic.

Acknowledgments

Many friends and colleagues have contributed suggestions and comments without which this book would never have been completed. In particular, I wish to acknowledge the help of Desmond Allison, Tracy de Gavilanes, Jean

Lehman, Emily Lites, and Richard Webber with the preparation of the manuscript. A special vote of thanks goes to Paul Martin for providing the illustrations. I would also like to thank past and present members of the faculty and staff of the Economics Institute, University of Colorado, and the Pre-Entry Science Department, University of Botswana, for their encouragement and support during the writing of this book.

SKILLS UNITS SCOPE AND SEQUENCE CHART

	Unit 1	Unit 3	Unit 5	Unit 7
WORD STUDY Context Clues	Identifying contextual definitions	Recognizing examples and restatements as context clues	Identifying synonyms and antonyms in context	Using context clues (review)
Stems and Affixes	Identifying parts of speech from affixes	Recognizing meanings of suffixes and prefixes	Recognizing prefixes with opposite meanings	Recognizing common word stems
Dictionary Use	Finding definitions of words in the dictionary	Choosing among multiple definitions	Using parts of speech to select appropriate definitions	Finding appropriate definitions (review)
SENTENCE STUDY Sentence Analysis	Locating main verb, subject and object or complement; recognizing signal words (conjunctions)	Locating pronoun antecedents; recognizing signal words (sentence connectors)	Identifying modifying clauses and phrases (with signal words)	Active and passive voice; finding main verb; identifying modifying phrases (no signal words)

(continued)

SKILLS UNITS SCOPE AND SEQUENCE CHART (Continued)

	Unit 1	Unit 3	Unit 5	Unit 7
Sentence Synthesis	Recognizing synonymous sentences (word order)	Recognizing synonymous sentence elements	Recognizing synonymous sentences (modifying clauses, phrases, signal words)	Simplifying complex sentences
PARAGRAPH STUDY Paragraph Analysis	Identifying the topic	Recognizing appropriate main idea	Identifying topic sentences	Recognizing paragraph development patterns
Paragraph Synthesis (Information Transfer)	Dividing information under subtopics	Dividing information according to level of generality	Dividing information according to time, place, and causal relationships	Outlining

READING SPEED Eyespan	Rapid recognition of identical words and phrases	Rapid recognition of identical words and phrases	Rapid recognition of identical words and phrases, and of synonyms	Rapid recognition of synonymous sentences (active and passive, participles, infinitives, appositives)
Application	Recognizing key phrases in context	Recognizing organization of information under subtopics in a paragraph	Recognizing synonyms in context	Scanning lists and tables for specific information

UNIT 1 Reading Skills

WORD STUDY

1. Identifying Contextual Definitions
2. Identifying Parts of Speech from Suffixes
3. Finding the Meaning of a Word in the Dictionary

SENTENCE STUDY

1. Identifying the Main Verb, Its Subject, and Its Object or Complement
2. Recognizing Synonymous Sentences

PARAGRAPH STUDY

1. Identifying the Topic of a Paragraph
2. Dividing Information According to Subtopics

READING SPEED

1. Rapid Recognition of Identical Words and Phrases
2. Recognition of Key Phrases in Context

1

Word Study

Identifying Contextual Definitions

Sometimes a writer tells the meaning of a new word. In the following sentence, the writer tells the meaning of the word "solar":

Solar energy is energy from the sun.

This sentence is like a "sentence" in mathematics:

$$\underline{\text{Solar}} \; \underline{\text{energy}} \; \text{is} \; \underline{\text{energy}} \; \underline{\text{from the sun.}}$$
$$\text{A} + \text{B} \quad = \quad \text{B} \; + \quad \text{C}$$

What is the meaning of "solar"?

1. energy
2. the sun
3. from the sun

The correct answer is 3: "from the sun." Why is 3 correct?

EXPLANATION:

- A is "solar," B is "energy," and C is "from the sun."
- The sentence says, "A + B = B + C."
- B and B are the same, so we can say that A = C ("solar" and "from the sun" are the same).

$$\text{In other words, A} + \text{B} = \text{B} + \text{C}$$
$$\text{B} = \text{B}$$
$$\therefore \text{A} = \text{C}$$

Now look at this sentence. In this sentence, the writer tells the meaning of the word "energy."

$$\underline{\text{Solar}} \; \underline{\text{energy}} \quad (\underline{\text{power}} \; \underline{\text{from the sun}}) \; \text{has many uses.}$$
$$\text{A} + \text{B} \quad = \quad \text{D} \quad + \quad \text{C}$$

What is the meaning of "energy"?

1. power
2. from the sun
3. many uses

The correct answer is 1. "power."

EXPLANATION:

We know that A = C or "solar" is the same as "from the sun." This sentence says, "A + B = *D* + C." A and C are the same, so we can say that B and D are also the same.

In other words, A + B = D + C
$$A = C$$
$$\therefore B = D$$

Here are some more ways writers tell the meaning of new words:

- Your instructor, or teacher, will explain the lesson.
  (The writer tells us that the meaning of "instructor" is "teacher.")
- The answer is in the conclusion, the last part of the story.
  (The writer tells that the meaning of "conclusion" is "the last part of the story.")
- People who study the stars are called astronomers.
  (The writer tells that the meaning of "astronomers" is "people who study the stars.")
- I will use diagrams—pictures or drawings—to explain the new machine.
  (The writer tells us that the meaning of "diagrams" is "pictures or drawings.")

Exercise 1–1

Directions: *Here are some more sentences. Read the sentences and answer the questions. Please do not use your dictionary.*

1. A hypothesis is a special kind of guess.

   What is the meaning of hypothesis?

   a. kind

   b. special

   c. a special kind of guess

2. Astronomers observe, or look at, the stars.

   What is the meaning of observe?

   a. look at

   b. the stars

   c. astronomers

3. Blind people (people who cannot see) have a difficult life.

   What is the meaning of blind?

   a. people

   b. who cannot see

   c. difficult

4. Scientists use a special <u>method</u>, or way of doing things, in their work.

   What is the meaning of <u>method</u>?

   a. their work

   b. special way

   c. way of doing things

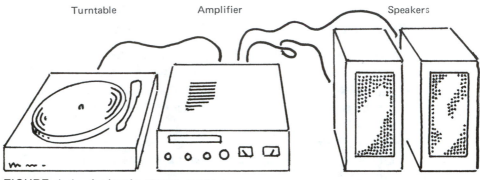

FIGURE 1-1   A simple stereo system

5. There are four parts, or <u>components</u>, in a simple stereo system.

   What is the meaning of <u>components</u>?

   a. parts

   b. simple

   c. stereo system

Sometimes a writer gives information about the meaning of a new word. A good reader looks for this information and uses it to guess the meaning of the new word. In the following sentences, the writer gives us information about the meaning of the word <u>normal</u>:

> Our teacher speaks in a special way in class, but he speaks in a <u>normal</u> way to his family. In class, he speaks English very slowly and <u>carefully</u> because we do not understand English well. However, he does not speak English slowly and carefully to his family because they can understand English very well.

What is the meaning of <u>normal</u>?

   a. slow and careful

   b. not special

   c. to his family

(The correct answer is b. "not special.")

EXPLANATION:

Answer a. is not correct because the teacher speaks in a *special* way (slowly and carefully) in class. Answer b. is correct because the teacher speaks in a <u>normal</u> way (not slowly and carefully) to his family, so we can guess that <u>normal</u> means "not special." Answer c. is not correct because <u>normal</u> tells about the way the teacher speaks, but "to his family" tells where he speaks in this way.

Exercise 1–2

Directions: *Here are some more sentences. Look for information about the meanings of the underlined words. Guess the meanings of the underlined words and find the* best *answer for each question. Please do* not *use your dictionary.*

1. Some cloth is made from <u>natural</u> fibers; some cloth is made from <u>synthetic</u> fibers. Natural fibers, such as cotton and wool, come from plants or animals. Nylon and polyester are called synthetic fibers because they are made by man.

   What is the meaning of <u>natural</u> in these sentences?

   a. made by man

   b. cotton and wool

   c. from plants or animals

   What is the meaning of <u>synthetic</u> in these sentences?

   a. made by man

   b. nylon and polyester

   c. from plants or animals

2. University students must read books, journals, reports, and many other <u>materials</u> in their studies.

   What is the meaning of <u>materials</u> in this sentence?

   a. books

   b. students

   c. things to read

3. Computers have many <u>uses</u>. Computers can solve problems. Computers can control machines. You can play games with computers and some computers can help you learn languages.

   What is the meaning of the <u>uses</u> of computers?

   a. things we can do with computers

   b. different types of computers

   c. computer games and languages

4. The Earth consists of land, air, and water. Water (H$_2$O) consists of two parts hydrogen (H$_2$) and one part oxygen (O).

   Look at the diagram on page 4. What does a simple stereo system consist of?

   a. a turntable

   b. four components

   c. two speakers

5. The numbers 0, 1, 2, 3, 4, 5, 6, 7, 8, and 9 are called digits. All numbers consist of one or more digits. For example, 8 is a one-digit number, 21 is a two-digit number, and 484 is a three-digit number.

   The number 10,125 is a _____ number.

   a. digit

   b. four-digit

   c. five-digit

6. Christopher Columbus observed an interesting phenomenon. When a ship was coming into port, at first he saw only the top part of the ship. Then he saw the top and middle parts of the ship, and finally all of it. This phenomenon gave Columbus the idea that the Earth is round like a ball.

   What is the phenomenon that Columbus observed?

   a. Columbus saw that a ship was coming into port.

   b. He saw first the top, then the middle, and finally all of the ship

   c. Columbus knew that the Earth was round like a ball.

7. Pollution is a serious problem in our city. Cars and factories put dangerous gases into the air. Some companies put dangerous chemicals into the water of our rivers and lakes. Pollution is also bad for the farmland around the city.

   What is the meaning of pollution in these sentences?

   a. cars and factories in our city

   b. air, water, and land around the city

   c. dangerous gases and chemicals

8. Pollution comes from many different sources. In our city most of the pollution in the air comes from cars. Pollution of the rivers comes from factories beside the rivers. Pollution of the land comes from smoke and gases in the air, and from chemicals in the water.

   What is the meaning of sources in these sentences?

   a. where something comes from

   b. smoke and gases in the air

   c. factories beside the rivers

Identifying Parts of Speech from Suffixes

Nouns and Verbs: All languages have nouns and verbs. A noun names a person, a place, a thing, an idea, an action, or a feeling. In a sentence, a noun can be a subject or an object. A verb tells what the subject is, does, or feels. Every sentence has a verb.

EXAMPLE:

```
        (noun)        (verb)        (noun)
An astronomer    observes   the stars.
  (subject)       (verb)             (object)
```

There are two nouns in this sentence: "astronomer" and "stars." "Astronomer" is the subject of the sentence. "Stars" is the object. The verb in this sentence is "observes." It tells what the subject (an astronomer) does.

In English, some words have the same form for nouns and verbs.

EXAMPLE:

```
            (verb)
You must answer the questions.

            (noun)
What is the answer?
```

Some words have different forms for nouns and verbs.

EXAMPLE:

```
                    (noun)
Astronomers make stellar observations.
            (verb)
An astronomer observes the stars.
```

Look at the noun and verb forms of these words:

Noun	Verb
observation	observe
explanation	explain
conclusion	conclude
collection	collect
pollution	pollute

The noun forms of these words have the same suffix, or ending. These nouns all end with the suffix "-ion."

Exercise 1-3

Directions: *Look at these sentences. Is the underlined word a noun or a verb? Write "noun" or "verb" in the space. The first one is done for you.*

1. Good readers <u>guess</u> the meanings of new words.

   _____*verb*_____

2. Computers have many <u>uses</u>. _____

3. Scientists <u>use</u> a special method in their work. _____

4. A hypothesis is a special kind of <u>guess</u>. _____

5. The diagram <u>explains</u> this phenomenon. _____

6. The sun <u>heats</u> the water in the swimming pool.

   _____

7. Please <u>print</u> your name here: _____

8. Did you understand the <u>explanation</u>? _____

9. Can you read the small <u>print</u>? _____

10. The teacher will <u>collect</u> the papers at the end of the class.

    _____

11. The <u>heat</u> of the sun makes the water hot. _____

12. She has a large <u>collection</u> of stamps. _____

Agent Nouns: Some nouns are called "agent nouns." An agent noun names a person or thing that does something. For example, a *reader* is a person who reads, and a *collector* is a person or thing that collects something.

Exercise 1-4

Directions: *Complete these sentences. The first one is done for you.*

1. A reader is a person who _____*reads*_____.

2. A teacher is a person who _____.

3. A _____ is a person who works.

4. A writer is a person who _____.

5. A _____ is a person who speaks.

6. An opener is a thing that _____ something.

7. A calculator is a thing that _____ arithmetic problems.

8. A _____ is a thing that synthesizes something.

9. A solar _____ is a thing that collects solar energy.

10. A scanner is a thing that _____, or looks at, something.

The agent nouns in Exercise 1–4 all end with the suffix "-er" or "-or." Some agent nouns have different suffixes. For example, a scien*tist* is a person who works in the field of science, and an account*ant* is a person who works in the field of accounting.

Suffix	Example
-er	reader
-or	calculator
-ist	scientist
-ian	technician
-ant	accountant
-ent	student

Exercise 1–5

Directions: *Complete these sentences. The first one is done for you.*

1. A person who studies is called a _____*student*_____.

2. A person who works in the field of science is called a

_____.

3. A person who works in the field of physics is called a

_____.

4. A person who works in a _____ field is called a specialist.

5. A person who works in a _____ field is called a technician.

Adjectives: An *adjective* is a modifying word. It gives us information about a noun. In English, most adjectives come before a noun, or after the verb "be."

EXAMPLES:

I have a *new* watch.

The weather is *hot*.

In the first sentence, "new" gives us information about the noun "watch." In the second sentence, "hot" gives us information about "the weather."

Exercise 1-6

Directions: *Look at these sentences and find the adjectives. Underline the adjective in each sentence. The first one is done for you.*

1. It is a digital watch.
2. Polyester is a synthetic fiber.
3. That snake is dangerous.
4. Solar energy is energy from the sun.
5. The sun is very hot today.
6. Scientists use a scientific method in their work.
7. A specialist is a person who works in a special field.
8. The teacher is speaking in a normal voice.

Look at the noun and adjective forms of these words:

Noun	Adjective
base	basic
science	scientific
nature	natural
digit	digital
danger	dangerous
number	numerous
expense	expensive
action	active

The adjective forms of these words have *adjective suffixes*. The suffixes "-ic," "-al," "-ous," and "-ive" are adjective suffices.

Exercise 1-7

Directions: *Look at these sentences. Is the underlined word a noun, a verb, or an adjective? Write "noun," "verb," or "adjective" in the space. The first one is done for you.*

1. He has a large collection of stamps. _____*noun*_____
2. The scientist forms a hypothesis. _____
3. Computers can solve mathematical problems. _____

4. Picasso is a famous artist. _____

5. Our calculations are always accurate. _____

6. Bruce Lee is a famous movie star. _____

7. The observer will watch you. _____

8. What is the correct form of this word? _____

9. Pollution is a problem in our city. _____

10. This is a basic English class. _____

Exercise 1-8

Directions: *Look at these words. All of the words end with suffixes. Circle the suffix of each word and write "noun" or "adjective" in the space. The first one is done for you.*

1. natural _____ ***adjective*** _____

2. calculation _____

3. economist _____

4. various _____

5. energetic _____

6. normal _____

7. computer _____

8. conclusive _____

Finding the Meaning of a Word in the Dictionary

Dictionaries are very important for students of English as a second language. Most students use two dictionaries: a bilingual dictionary and an English dictionary. A bilingual dictionary tells you the meanings of English words in your own language. An English dictionary tells you the meanings of English words in English. An English dictionary also gives you information about the pronunciation, spelling, and forms of English words.

Alphabetical Order: Words in an English dictionary are in *alphabetical order.* They follow the order of the alphabet (a, b, c, d, e, f, g, etc.). For example, "answer" comes before "basic" in the dictionary because "a" comes before "b" in the alphabet. "Cell" comes before "correct" because "e" comes before "o." "Danger" comes before "daylight" because "n" comes before "y."

Exercise 1-9

Directions: *The words in this list are not in alphabetical order. Write the words in alphabetical order in the spaces provided. The first two are done for you.*

collect	guess	analyze
reason	expensive	signal
perform	pollution	complex
explain	power	control

1. _____*analyze*_____   5. _____   9. _____

2. _____*collect*_____   6. _____   10. _____

3. _____   7. _____   11. _____

4. _____   8. _____   12. _____

Dictionary Guide Words: Open your English dictionary and look at the two words at the top of each page. These two words are called *guide words*. The first guide word is the first word on the page, and the second guide word is the last word on the page.

Guide words help you find a word in the dictionary quickly. For example, I am looking for the word "feel" in my dictionary. On page 400, the guide words are "favor" and "feed." On page 401 the guide words are "fend off" and "fiber." I know I can find the word "feel" on page 401 because "feel" comes between "feed" and "fender" in alphabetical order.

Exercise 1-10

Directions: *Here is a list of words. Three of these words are on page 400 in my dictionary, three words are on page 401, and three words are on page 402. Look at the guide words and find the correct page for each word. Write the words in the correct spaces. The first one is done for you.*

fiasco

feet

(feature) ─────────────┐

federal

fellow

fence

favor	400	feed
feature		
_____		
_____		

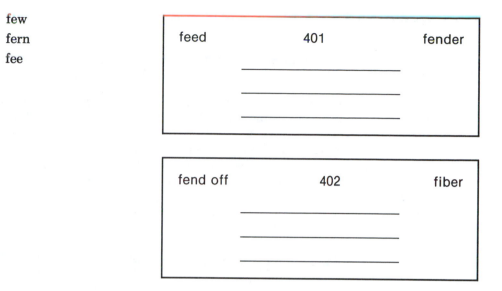

few
fern
fee

feed	401	fender

fend off	402	fiber

Using the Dictionary

Exercise 1–11

Directions: *Look at the words in this list. How many of these words do you know? How many of these words are new words? Put a check (✔) beside the words you know.*

_____ phenomenon	_____ computer	_____ analyze
_____ reason	_____ problem	_____ recognize
_____ experiment	_____ danger	_____ explain
_____ pollution	_____ collect	_____ form
_____ power	_____ perform	_____ guess
_____ voice	_____ touch	_____ expensive
_____ signal	_____ solve	_____ complex
_____ library	_____ control	_____ aloud

Now find the meanings of the new words (words you do not know) in your English dictionary. Use the guide words to find the words quickly. If you do not understand the definition, or meaning of the word, find the meaning in your bilingual dictionary. Then write a sentence with the new word. This will help you to remember the word. Compare your sentences with the sentences of the other students in your class. This will help you to learn more about the meanings of the new words.

Sentence Study

Identifying the Main Verb, Its Subject and Its Object or Complement

SVO Sentences: Most English sentences have three parts: a subject, a verb, and an object or complement. These sentences are called SVO sentences. (S = subject, V = verb, O = object or complement.)*

In order to find the three parts of an SVO sentence, first find the verb. Sometimes the verb is one word. Sometimes there are other words with the verb like "is," "are," "have," "has," "can," "may," etc. After you find the verb, look for the subject. The subject usually comes before the verb. Last, find the object or complement. The object or complement comes after the verb.

EXAMPLE:

Industrial <u>pollution</u> <u>causes</u> many <u>problems</u>.
                S   V   O

In this sentence, the verb is one word: "causes." The subject is "pollution." It comes before the verb. The word "industrial" is an adjective. It gives us information about the subject, but it is not the subject. The object of this sentence is "problems." It comes before the verb. The word "many" is a quantifier, or number word. It gives us information about the object, but it is not the object.

Exercise 1–12

Directions: *Look at these sentences. Find the verb, the subject, and the object or complement in each sentence. Write "S" above the subject, "V" above the verb, and "O" above the object or complement. The first one is done for you.*

               S   **V**   **O**
1. The <u>library</u> is <u>collecting</u> more <u>materials</u>.
2. Most sentences have three parts.
3. Scientists perform experiments.
4. Large computers can solve complex problems.
5. Our engineers will test the new calculators.
6. The students in this class are learning English.

*Some English sentences do not have a subject, and some sentences do not have an object or complement. Imperative sentences like "Answer the question!" do not have a subject, and sentences like "Children play." do not have an object or complement.

SVO + SVO Sentences: Sometimes a writer joins two sentences together. Writers use signal words—words like "and," "but," and "however"—to join the sentences. Signal words tell us about the two sentences. "And" and "also" tell us that the second sentence will give more information about the first sentence. "But" and "however" tell us that the second sentence will have different information from the first sentence.

EXAMPLES:

His sister gave him a watch for his birthday, *and* his brother gave him a book.

(The second sentence has *more* information about the gifts he received for his birthday.)

His sister gave him a watch for his birthday, *but* his brother gave him nothing.

(The second sentence has *different* information about the gifts he received for his birthday.)

Exercise 1–13

Directions: *Look at these sentences. Find the signal words. Underline the signal word in each sentence. Does the second sentence give* more *information or* different *information about the first sentence? Write "more" or "different" in the space. The first one is done for you.*

1. His mother remembered his birthday; <u>however</u>, his father forgot it.

   _____*different*_____ information

2. The farmers grow food, and the people in the cities eat it.

   _____ information

3. New York City is a large city, but Woodstock, New York is a small town.

   _____ information

4. You can buy medicine at a drug store; you can also buy magazines, books, film, toys, and many other goods there.

   _____ information

5. I am from Uruguay; my husband, however, is from the United States.

   _____ information

$S {\Large\langle} \begin{smallmatrix} VO \\ \\ VO \end{smallmatrix}$ *Sentences* and $\begin{smallmatrix} S \\ \\ S \end{smallmatrix} {\Large\rangle} VO$ *Sentences:* Some sentences have one subject and two or more verbs. This happens when a writer joins two sentences with the same subject, and the writer does not want to write the same subject two times.

EXAMPLE:

A. The secretary lives in Virginia.

B. The secretary works in Washington.

A + B: The secretary lives in Virginia and works in Washington.

$$S \Big< \begin{matrix} \text{VO} \\ \text{VO} \end{matrix} \quad \text{The secretary} \Big< \begin{matrix} \text{lives in Virginia} \\ \text{and} \\ \text{works in Washington} \end{matrix}$$

Some sentences have one verb and two or more subjects. This happens when a writer joins two sentences with the same verb, and the writer does not want to write the same verb two times.

EXAMPLE:

A. Scientists work in the laboratory.

B. Technicians work in the laboratory.

A + B: Scientists and technicians work in the laboratory.

$$\begin{matrix} S \\ S \end{matrix} \Big> \text{VO} \quad \begin{matrix} \text{Scientists} \\ \text{and} \\ \text{Technicians} \end{matrix} \Big> \text{work in the laboratory}$$

Exercise 1–14

Directions: *Look at these sentences. Find the subjects and verbs of the sentences. Some sentences have one subject and one verb (SVO). Some sentences have two subjects and two verbs (SVO + SVO). Some sentences have one subject and two verbs (S $\substack{\text{VO} \\ \text{VO}}$), and some sentences have two subjects and one verb ($\substack{\text{S} \\ \text{S}}$ VO). Write the subjects and verbs in the spaces. The first one is done for you.*

1. Commuters live in the suburbs and work in the cities.

   Subjects: ___*Commuters*___   Verbs: ___*live*___

   _____   ___*work*___

2. Scientists make observations and perform experiments.

   Subjects: _____   Verbs: _____

   _____   _____

3. This writer uses many new words.

Subjects: _____   Verbs: _____

_____   _____

4. The receptionist answers the telephone, and the secretary types the letters.

Subjects: _____   Verbs: _____

_____   _____

5. The observer collects information and sends reports to the Capitol.

Subjects: _____   Verbs: _____

_____   _____

6. Blind people can recognize voices and identify sounds.

Subjects: _____   Verbs: _____

_____   _____

7. Many people know about solar energy, but few people use it.

Subjects: _____   Verbs: _____

_____   _____

8. The teacher and the students are speaking English.

Subjects: _____   Verbs: _____

_____   _____

9. Astronomers and physicists are scientists.

Subjects: _____   Verbs: _____

_____   _____

10. Energy comes from many sources.

Subjects: _____   Verbs: _____

_____   _____

Recognizing Synonymous Sentences

Sometimes different sentences have the same meaning. For example, these three sentences have the same meaning:

I use a pen to write letters.

I use a pen for writing letters.

I write letters with a pen.

A writer can change the place of some words in a sentence. Usually this does not change the meaning. For example, these sentences have the same meaning:

I use a pen to write letters.

To write letters, I use a pen.

Sometimes, changing the place of some words in a sentence changes the meaning of the sentence. For example, these sentences do *not* have the same meaning:

I use a pen to write letters.

I write letters to use a pen.

Exercise 1–15

Directions: *Look at these groups of sentences. One sentence has the same meaning as the first sentence in the group. Find the sentence with the same meaning and put a check (✓) beside it. The first one is done for you. After you finish, discuss your answers with the other students in your class.*

1. We use solar energy to produce electricity for our house.

   _____ a. Our house uses electricity to produce solar energy.

   __✓__ b. We produce electricity for our house with solar energy.

   _____ c. We use electricity for solar energy in our house.

   EXPLANATION:
   The correct answer is "b" because "produce electricity with solar energy" has the same meaning as "use solar energy to produce electricity."

2. To test the hypothesis, the scientist will perform an experiment.

   _____ a. The scientist will perform an experiment to test the hypothesis.

   _____ b. The scientist will test a hypothesis to perform an experiment.

   _____ c. The hypothesis will perform an experiment to test the scientist.

3. A used car is less expensive than a new car.

   _____ a. A used car is more expensive than a new car.

   _____ b. A used car is as expensive as a new car.

   _____ c. A new car is more expensive than a used car.

4. Airplanes are not as dangerous as motorcycles.

　　———　a. Airplanes are more dangerous than motorcycles.

　　———　b. Airplanes are less dangerous than motorcycles.

　　———　c. Motorcycles are as dangerous as airplanes.

5. Blind people must learn a special alphabet in order to read.

　　———　a. For reading, blind people must learn a special alphabet.

　　———　b. For blind people to learn, a special alphabet must be read.

　　———　c. To learn a special alphabet, blind people must read.

6. A calculator can help a student solve a problem quickly; however, the student must understand the problem first.

　　———　a. A calculator helps a student solve and understand problems quickly.

　　———　b. With a calculator, a student can answer a problem quickly, but first he or she must understand the problem.

　　———　c. A student can solve a problem quickly, and then the student can understand the problem with a calculator.

Paragraph Study

Identifying the Topic of a Paragraph

A paragraph is a group of sentences. The first sentence is a paragraph usually begins about five spaces inside the margin. A paragraph looks like this:

(First sentence) _____

_____ . (Second sentence) _____

_____ . (Third sentence) _____

_____ .

(Fourth sentence) _____ . (Fifth

sentence) _____ .

All the sentences in a paragraph are about one thing, the *topic* of the paragraph. It tells us about the kind of information in the paragraph.

EXAMPLE:

Read this paragraph and find the topic.

The people in the United States speak the same language as the people in Great Britain. However, American English is different from British English in many ways. First, the sounds of American English are different from the sounds of British English. For example, most Americans pronounce the "r" in the word "car" but most Britons do not. Most Americans pronounce the word "dictionary" like this: " 'dik-shun-,ar-y," but the British pronounce it like this " 'dik-shun-ry." Some spellings are also different. People in Britain write "colour" and "centre," but people in the United States write "color" and "center." Finally, some words are different. People in the United States use "gasoline" in their cars, but people in Britain use "petrol." Gasoline and petrol are the same thing, but the Americans and the British use different words for it.

What is the topic of this paragraph?

a. American English
b. the English language
c. the different sounds of American and British English
d. the differences between American and British English

(The correct answer is "d. the differences between American and British English.")

EXPLANATION:

Answer a. is not correct because the paragraph is about American English *and* British English, not only American English. Answer b. is not correct because the paragraph is about two kinds of English: American and British. It is not about *all* of the English language. Answer c. is not correct because the paragraph is about the different sounds, spellings, and words in American and British English. Only three sentences are about the different *sounds*. Answer d. is correct because the paragraph is about both American and British English, and about the differences between them.

Exercise 1-16

Directions: *Now read the following paragraphs and answer the questions. After you finish, discuss your answers with other students in your class.*

PARAGRAPH 1

Do you have trouble remembering new words in English? Many people have this problem. This method may help you to remember new words. (1)

Look at the new word. Look at the letters and the shape of the word. Close your eyes. Can you see the word? (2) Listen to the word. Listen to the sounds in the word. Look at the word as you listen. (3) Say the word aloud. Close your book. Do not look at the word. Can you say it? (4) Write the word. Write it three or four times. Say the word as you write it. (5) Use the new word. Use it in class today, and use it at home tonight. Use it tomorrow and next week. Look for the new word in the newspaper and listen for it on the radio or on television. To remember a new word, you must use it.

What is the topic of this paragraph?

a. a method for remembering new words

b. new words in English

c. looking at new words

d. the uses of new words in English

PARAGRAPH 2

Computer chips have changed our way of life. With computer chips we can make very small computers. Space scientists use these small computers in satellites and space ships. Large companies use these small computers for business. We can make very small calculators with computer chips. Some calculators are as small as a credit card, and these calculators are not very expensive. Computer chips are also used for making digital watches. A normal watch has a spring and moving hands, but a digital watch has no moving parts. A digital watch shows the time and the date with numbers, and some digital watches even have an alarm and a stop-watch. The computer chip makes all of this possible.

What is the topic of this paragraph?

a. small computers

b. uses of computer chips

c. digital watches

d. uses of computers

PARAGRAPH 3

Today most cars use gasoline, but in the future many people may drive electric cars. Electric cars do not pollute the air. Electricity from a battery powers the motor of an electric car. Drivers of electric cars do not fill their cars with gasoline; they connect their cars to an electrical outlet to charge the battery with electricity. The driver of an electric car connects the car to an electrical outlet at night. In the morning, the battery is charged with enough electricity to drive all day. Electric cars are not as fast as gasoline-powered cars, and they cannot travel more than 150 miles (270 kilometers). After 150 miles, the driver must charge the battery again. However, electric cars may be one answer to the problems of pollution and high gasoline prices.

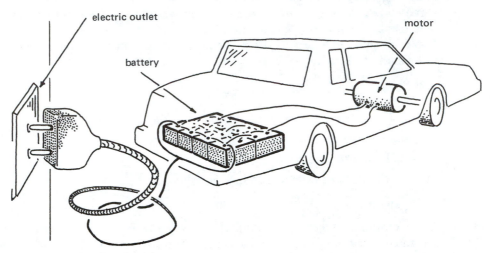

FIGURE 1–2   An electric car

What is the topic of this paragraph?

a. pollution and expensive gasoline
b. the batteries of electric cars
c. gasoline cars
d. electric cars

Dividing Information According to Subtopics

A paragraph has only one topic, but sometimes the topic has two or more *subtopics*. These subtopics are part of the main topic. "Sub" means "under," so we say that the subtopics come under the main topic.

EXAMPLE:

Look at the paragraph on page 20. The topic of this paragraph is "the differences between American and British English." The three *subtopics* under this main topic are "sounds," "spellings," and "words".

TOPIC: Differences between American and British English

SUBTOPICS: 1. sounds
2. spellings
3. words

The writer organizes the information in the paragraph under the topic and the three subtopics like this:

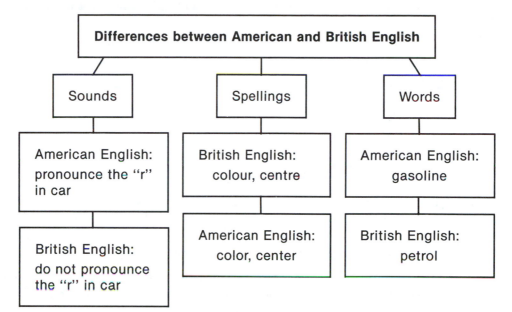

Exercise 1-17

Directions: *Look at Paragraph 1 and Paragraph 2 in Exercise 1-16. Find the subtopics of each paragraph and write them in the spaces.*

PARAGRAPH 1

TOPIC: a method for remembering new words

SUBTOPICS: 1. _____

2. _____

3. _____

4. _____

5. _____

PARAGRAPH 2

TOPIC: uses of computer chips

SUBTOPICS: 1. _____

2. _____

3. _____

Now look at Paragraph 3. The topic of Paragraph 3 is "electric cars," and the paragraph tells us four things that electric cars do *not* do. Find the four things that electric cars do not do and write them in the spaces.

TOPIC: electric cars

1. They do not use _____.

2. They do not make _____.

3. They are not _____.

4. They cannot _____.

Reading Speed

Rapid Recognition of Identical Words and Phrases

Recognizing Words Quickly: Good readers can read quickly. When you read quickly, you can read more and you can understand better. An important part of reading quickly is recognizing words quickly. Sometimes different words *look* similar. For example, "hot" and "not" look similar but they are different. Sometimes different words *sound* similar. For example, "hat" and "had" sound similar but they are different.

This exercise will help you to recognize words quickly. It will help you to find the differences between words that look or sound similar.

Exercise 1–18

Directions: *Look at the first word. Then look at the other words on the same line. Find the first word and circle it.*

EXAMPLE:

hot   not   cot   had   hat   (hot)   hut   not

Read as quickly as you can. Try to finish in the suggested time. After you finish, trade books with another student in your class and check his or her answers.

1. (suggested time: 30 seconds)

heat	head	heel	hit	heat	heal	head	hate
form	farm	form	firm	from	frame	farm	fern
send	sand	sent	sound	sent	sand	send	mend

wind	wend	went	wind	wound	wild	went	word
rays	rays	raise	trays	rise	stays	says	race
add	and	end	old	odd	aid	add	and
eyes	yes	ice	eyes	eves	says	ewes	yes
test	text	taste	list	lost	last	text	test
blind	blink	bind	blind	blonde	bland	blend	
guess	guest	quest	gust	guess	dress	egress	
voice	vice	vocal	boys	vase	voice	voice	wise
power	powder	pourer	power	plover	powder	pour	
solve	salve	slave	solve	shelve	stave	shave	
charge	chance	change	large	cringe	charge	orange	

2. (suggested time: 30 seconds)

source	sauce	scarce	source	scour	scarce	
computer	computer	compute	commuter	composer		
perform	perfect	inform	pretend	profound	perform	
normal	natural	narrow	normal	normalcy	numeral	
collect	collect	connect	correct	collection		
expensive	expressive	expansive	expensive	explosive		
storage	shortage	salvage	storage	stove	steerage	
aloud	loud	allowed	load	aloud	alone	along
control	contract	control	central	complex	contrast	
signal	single	singer	several	signal	signed	
brain	brain	train	strain	brand	brine	blind

3. (suggested time: 30 seconds)

scientist	science	scientific	scientist	scenarist	
electric	electricity	electic	electric	ecentric	
collector	collection	collector	collection	collecting	
observes	observer	observation	observed	observes	obscures
calculator	calculate	calculation	calculator	calculated	

synthetic   synthesize   synthesis   synthesizer   synthetic

analyze   analyze   analyst   analysis   analytic   catalyst

conclusion   conclusive   conclude   concluded   conclusion

uses   used   useless   user   uses   use   useful

natural   nature   national   naturalist   natural   natal

pollution   polluted   pollution   pollutant   pollutes   polluter

mathematical   mathematics   mathematician   mathematical   medical

Recognizing Phrases Quickly: Another part of reading quickly is recognizing phrases quickly. A phrase is group of two or more words. Slow readers read word-by-word, but good readers read phrase-by-phrase.

EXAMPLES:

When you read word-by-word, you read like this:

Slow   readers   read   word   by   word.

When you read phrase-by-phrase, you read like this:

Good readers   can read   phrase-by-phrase.

These exercises will help you to recognize phrases quickly. They will help you to read phrase-by-phrase.

Exercise 1–19

Directions: *Look at the key phrase. Then look at the other phrases in the list. Find the key phrase and circle it. You may find the key phrase more than one time. Read as quickly as you can and try to finish in the suggested time.*

EXAMPLE:

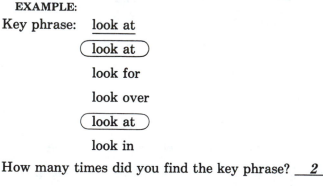

Key phrase: look at

look at

look for

look over

look at

look in

How many times did you find the key phrase?   *2*

1. Key phrase: consists of   (suggested time: 30 seconds)

   contents of

   consists of

composed of

contest for

consent to

consist of

contrast to

consists of

contents of

comprised of

consists of

contents of

composed of

comes from

consists of

How many times did you find the key phrase? _____

2. Key phrase: <u>sources of energy</u>   (suggested time: 20 seconds)

sources of everything

sources of energy

consists of energy

sources of pollution

courses of energy

sources of energy

scarcity of energy

sources of danger

sources of analysis

signals of energy

sources of materials

sources of energy

sources of solar energy

energy resources

How many times did you find the key phrase? _____

3. Key phrase: <u>the meanings of words</u>   (suggested time: 20 seconds)

the meaning of a word

the making of words

the message of words

the meanings of words

the moving of words

the materials of work

the making of a word

the meaning of a word

the meanings of work

the meanings of words

the meanings of words

the uses of a word

the meaning of work

How many times did you find the key phrase? _____

Exercise 1–20

Directions: *Look at the key phrase. Then look at the other phrases in the "paragraph." Find the key phrase and circle it. You may find the key phrase more than one time in the "paragraph."*

EXAMPLE:

Key phrase: **consists of**

contents of   composed of   (consists of)   content to

consisted of   exist for   contest for   (consists of)   composed

of   (consists of)   content to   composed of   contents of

composed of   (consists of)   contend for

How many times did you find the key phrase? _**4**_

1. Key phrase: **is called** (suggested time: 40 seconds)

is called   his cold   has called   is called   was cold

this call   is pulled   was killed   is walled   his wallet   this

caller   is called   was called   if called   is tall   his call

is called   in all   so tall   is calling   was called   is called
was walled   is calling   is called

How many times did you find the key phrase? _____

2. Key phrase: **in conclusion** (suggested time: 40 seconds)

is conclusive   in conclusion   in collection   is collected
if concluded   is concluded   in conclusion   in collusion   in
concord   in compulsion   in collision   in conclusion   in
conclusion   is conclusive   is collusive   if cohesive   in
cohesion   in conclusion   is conclusive   is compulsive   in
collection   in correction   in conclusion

How many times did you find the key phrase? _____

3. Key phrase: **a special method** (suggested time: 30 seconds)

a social method   a special method   a specific method
a special material   especially modern   a social method   the
scientific method   a special method   a social method   a special
model   a specific method   a special reason   a special method
a special method   a social model   a special method   a specific
method   a scientific model

How many times did you find the key phrase? _____

4. Key phrase: **a large number** (suggested time: 30 seconds)

a large number   a long number   a large member   a large
number   a larger number   a longer number   a long number   a
large number   a lengthy number   a large sum   a longer sum   a
loud number   a large number   a small number   a large member
a long name   a large name   a large number   a loud member

How many times did you find the key phrase? _____

5. Key phrase: **with their fingers** (suggested time: 30 seconds)

with the family   with their fingers   withered fingers
with the wringer   with their fingers   with the winter   with

their fingers   with their fingers   with the finger   with their
family   both their fingers   with other singers   with these
fingers   with other fingers   with their fingers   with tiny
fingers   with their fingers   with their letters   withered
fingers   winter fingers

How many times did you find the key phrase? _____

Recognizing Key Phrases in Context

Students often look for key phrases in their textbooks when they are reading, or when they are studying for a test. This exercise will help you find key phrases quickly.

Exercise 1-21

Directions: *Find the three paragraphs in Exercise 1-16 (on pages 20-22). Look at the key phrase for each of the following paragraphs. Then look for the key phrase in the paragraph and underline it. You will find the key phrase more than one time. When you finish, write in the spaced provided how many times you found the key phrase. Try to do this exercise as quickly as you can.*

PARAGRAPH 1

Key phrase: **the new word**

How many times did you find the key phrase? _____

PARAGRAPH 2

Key phrase: **computer chips**

How many times did you find the key phrase? _____

PARAGRAPH 3

Key phrase: **electric cars**

How many times did you find the key phrase? _____

UNIT 2 Reading Passages

The Scientific Method of Reading

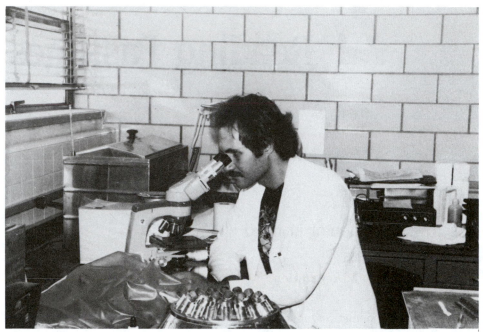

Photo by the author

Introduction

How do scientists do their work? They use a special method, or way of doing things. Students learn this method, the scientific method, in high school science classes.

How do students do their work? They also use a special method. Good students use a scientific method of studying. This method helps them to learn many things in a short time.

Reading is an important part of studying. This chapter is about a special method for reading, "The Scientific Method of Reading."

Vocabulary Preparation

This cartoon will help you understand some of the words in "The Scientific Method of Reading."

FIGURE 2-1   The Scientific Method

Text

The Scientific Method of Reading

Scientists use a special method in their work. This scientific method consists of four steps: observation, hypothesis, experiment, and conclusion.

STEP 1:   *Observation.* The scientist observes a phenomenon and collects information about the phenomenon.

STEP 2:   *Hypothesis.* The scientist forms a hypothesis. He or she guesses the reason for the phenomenon.

STEP 3:   *Experiment.* The scientist tests the hypothesis. He or she performs experiments and makes more observations.

STEP 4:   *Conclusion.* The scientist forms a conclusion. The hypothesis sometimes explains the phenomenon. Sometimes it does not. Then the scientist must form a new hypothesis or perform new experiments.

Good readers use a scientific method in their reading. They try to guess the meanings of new words.

STEP 1:   *Observation.* The reader looks at the word and looks at all the words and sentences around it.

STEP 2:   *Hypothesis.* The reader forms a hypothesis. He or she guesses the meaning of the word.

STEP 3:   *Experiment.* The reader tests the hypothesis. He or she tests the meaning in the sentence. He or she finds the word in different sentences and tests the meaning again.

STEP 4:   *Conclusion.* The reader forms a conclusion. The hypothesis sometimes explains the meaning of the word. Sometimes it does not. Then the reader must guess again or look in a dictionary.

Comprehension Questions

Directions: *Yes or no? Write "yes" or "no" in each space.*

1. Is the scientific method a special method? _____

2. Does the scientific method consists of three steps?

   _____

3. Does the hypothesis always explain the phenomenon?

   _____

4. Do good readers use a scientific method in their reading?

   _____

5. Do good readers guess the meaning of new words?

_____

Directions: *Choose the best answer.*

1. What special method do scientists use in their work?
   a. the phenomenon method
   b. the scientific method of reading
   c. the scientific method
   d. the conclusion method

2. How many steps does the scientific method consist of?
   a. 2 steps
   b. 4 steps
   c. 6 steps
   d. 8 steps

3. What is step 2 of the scientific method?
   a. observation
   b. conclusion
   c. experiment
   d. hypothesis

4. How does a scientist test the hypothesis?
   a. He or she performs an experiment.
   b. He or she guesses the meaning of a word.
   c. He or she finds the word in different sentences.
   d. He or she forms a conclusion.

5. How does a good reader test the hypothesis?
   a. He or she performs an experiment.
   b. He or she finds the word in different sentences.
   c. He or she guesses the meaning of the word.
   d. He or she forms a conclusion.

6. What is the topic of the first paragraph in the text?
   (Note: See Unit 1 Paragraph Study for explanations of "topic" and "paragraph.")
   a. scientists
   b. good readers
   c. the scientific method of reading
   d. the scientific method

Directions: *Find these sentences in the text. Look for the missing words and write them in the spaces.*

  EXAMPLE:

  Scientists use a _____*special*_____ method in their work.

1. The scientific method _____ of four steps.

2. The scientist _____ a phenomenon.

3. The scientist _____ a conclusion.

4. The reader forms a hypothesis. He or she _____ the meaning of the word.

5. The hypothesis _____ explains the meaning of the word. Sometimes it does _____ explain the meaning of the word.

6. The reader must _____ again or look in a

  _____.

Sun Power

Introduction

Energy comes from many sources. Most of our energy comes from oil. Gasoline for cars, trucks, and buses comes from oil. We also heat our food, our water, and our houses with oil and natural gas. However, oil is expensive and it causes pollution. Another source of energy is the nucleus of the atom. Nuclear power plants make electricity for many cities in the world, but nuclear power is expensive and dangerous.

Today, people are looking for different sources of energy. Some people are using wind power to make electricity. A few people are driving electric cars. Many people are using the sun as a source of energy. This chapter is about solar energy, or energy from the sun.

Vocabulary Preparation

Directions: *Look at the pictures and read the statements. Then write the correct words in the spaces.*

FIGURE 2-2 Energy comes from many sources

STATEMENTS: Solar energy is energy from the sun.
The sun is the source of solar energy.

Solar houses have a large number of windows to collect the heat of the sun.

Write the correct words in the spaces.

EXAMPLE:

_____*Solar*_____ energy = energy from the sun.

1. The sun = the _____ of solar energy.

2. Solar houses have many _____.

3. These windows collect the _____ of the sun.

FIGURE 2-3   Solar heat

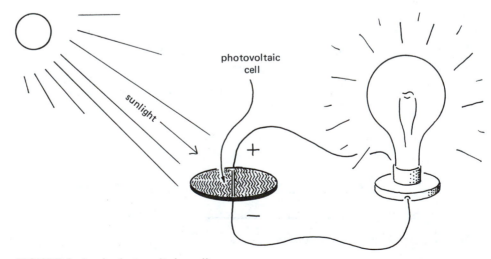

FIGURE 2-4   A photovoltaic cell

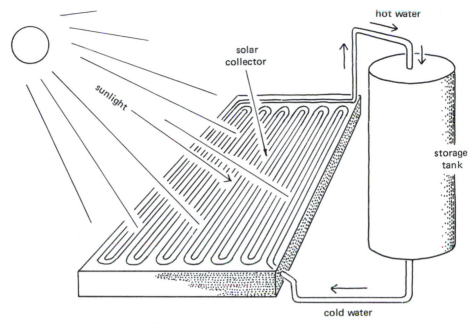

FIGURE 2-5 A solar collector

STATEMENTS: Photovoltaic cells change sunlight to electricity.

Solar collectors use sunlight to make hot water.

Write the correct words in the spaces.

1. Sunlight + _____ cells → electricity.

2. Sunlight + _____ collectors → electrcity.

3. A solar _____ makes hot water with sunlight.

4. A photovoltaic cell makes _____ from sunlight.

Text

Sun Power

Solar energy (power from the sun) has many uses. In many parts of the world, people are building solar houses with large numbers of windows to collect the heat of the sun. Solar collectors can make hot water from sunlight. The rays of the sun heat water in a solar collector, and the hot water goes into a storage tank. People can use the hot water for washing or for heating their houses. In the future, people may use the rays of the sun to make electricity for their homes. They will use photovoltaic cells to make electricity from sunlight.

The sun is an important "new" source of energy. It is less expensive than oil or nuclear energy. Furthermore, it does not cause pollution, and it is not as dangerous as nuclear power. Many people think that solar energy will be the answer to our future energy problems.

Comprehension Questions

Directions: *Yes or no? Write "yes" or "no" in the spaces.*

1. Does solar energy come from the sun? _____

2. Are people building houses on the sun? _____

3. Do many people make electricity for their houses with photovoltaic cells

   today? _____

4. Is solar energy less expensive than nuclear energy? _____

5. Does solar energy cause pollution? _____

Directions: *Choose the best answer.*

1. What is the source of solar energy?
   a. the earth   c. oil
   b. the sun   d. the nucleus

2. What can a solar collector do?
   a. It can answer our future energy problems.
   b. It can make electricity from sunlight.
   c. It can use hot water for washing.
   d. It can make hot water from sunlight.

3. Where are people building solar houses?
   a. in some places
   b. in all parts of the world
   c. in most countries in the world

4. What problems may solar energy solve?
   a. water shortages
   b. future energy problems
   c. storage problems

5. How do people use the hot water from a solar collector?
   a. for nuclear power   c. for washing and heating
   b. to cause pollution   d. to change sunlight into electricity

Directions: *What do you think? Write answers to these questions and discuss them with other students in your class.*

1. Is the sun a new source of energy?
2. When will people use photovoltaic cells for their houses?
3. Will solar energy be the answer to our energy problems?

Additional Reading

Sun Power

John and Marsha live in a solar house in New Mexico, a state in the Southwest of the United States. There are fifteen windows on the south wall of the house, and there are four solar collectors on the roof. Two of the solar collectors heat water for washing, and two collectors help to heat the house. In the winter, John and Marsha open the curtains on the south side of the house every morning, and they close them every evening. The rays of the sun heat the house during the day, and the curtains hold the heat in the house during the night. In the hot summer season, John and Marsha close the curtains during the day, and they turn off two of their solar collectors.

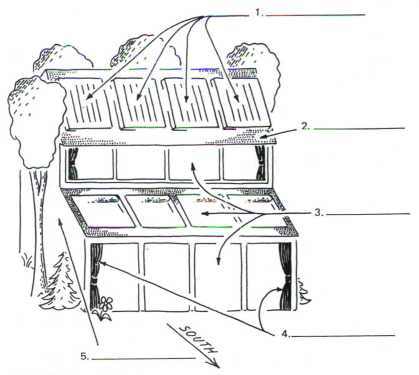

FIGURE 2–6   A solar house

Directions: *Figure 2-6 is a picture of John and Marsha's house. Label the parts of the house. Use these words: windows, roof, wall, curtains, solar collectors.*

Directions: *Choose the best answer.*

1. What is the topic of this paragraph? (Note: See Unit 1 Paragraph Study for an explanation of "topic.")
   a. John and Marsha
   b. New Mexico
   c. a solar house
   d. solar collectors
2. In the winter, what do John and Marsha do every morning?
   a. They close the curtains.
   b. They open the curtains.
   c. They turn off the solar collectors.
   d. They heat water for washing.
3. When do John and Marsha close the curtains in the morning?
   a. in the summer
   b. in the winter
   c. during the day
   d. at night
4. What do the curtains do at night in the winter?
   a. They heat the house.
   b. They heat water for washing.
   c. They turn off the solar collectors.
   d. They hold heat in the house.
5. Which solar collectors do John and Marsha turn off in the summer?
   a. the two collectors that heat water for washing
   b. the two collectors that help to heat the house
   c. all of the collectors

Directions: *What do you think? Try to answer these questions. Discuss your answers with other students in your class.*

1. Why do John and Marsha close the curtains during the day in summer?
2. Why are the windows on the *south* wall of the house?
3. New Mexico is in the *Northern Hemisphere*. In the *Southern*

Hemisphere, do solar houses have more windows on the south wall or the north wall?

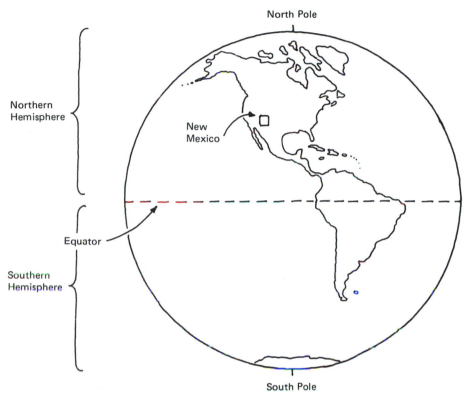

FIGURE 2-7   The hemispheres

Prereading Questions

Directions: *Try to answer these questions while you are reading the following paragraph.*

1. What is the problem with photovoltaic cells today?
2. How will photovoltaic cells change in the future?
3. How will photovoltaic cells be used in the future?

Photovoltaic cells were used in the U.S. space program in the 1960s and 1970s, and they have been making electricity for lights, refrigerators, and water pumps in the Arizona desert since 1979. In 1980, photovoltaic cells powered a small airplane named the *Gossamer Penguin;* and on July 7, 1981, another solar-powered airplane, the *Solar Challenger,* flew across the English Channel from France to England.

These cells are very expensive, and at least 6000 cells are necessary to make enough electricity for one house. Today, the cells are made from silicon crystals. Many cells are put together on a panel, the cells are connected with wires, and they are covered with glass. It is expensive to make photovoltaic cells this way, and it takes a long time. However, scientists are working on a new way to make many cells at the same time. It willl take less time to make the cells this way, and they wil be less expensive. In five or ten years, many houses in North America, Europe, and Japan will get all their electricity from photovoltaic cells.

Directions: *Here is a picture of a panel of photovoltaic cells. Label the parts. Use the words: silicon crystals, glass, wires.*

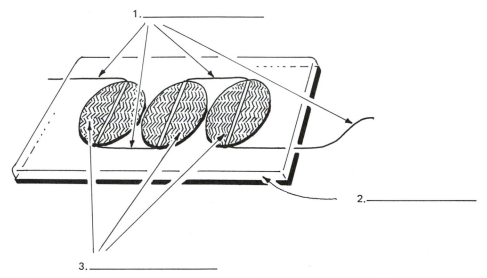

1. _____

2. _____

3. _____

FIGURE 2–8   A panel of photovoltaic cells

Directions: *Choose the best answer.*

1. What is the topic of this paragraph? (Note: See Unit 1 Paragraph Study for an explanation of "topic.")

   a. space programs
   b. the *Solar Challenger*
   c. photovoltaic cells
   d. solar energy

2. What are photovoltaic cells made from today?

   a. wires
   b. electricity

   c. glass panels

   d. silicon crystals

3. In the future, photovoltaic cells will be less expensive because

    ————————————.

   a. they will be made in a new way

   b. they are made from silicon crystals

   c. it takes a long time to make them

   d. one house needs 6000 cells

Directions: *What do you think? Write answers to these questions and discuss your answers with other students in your class.*

1. Why are photovoltaic cells expensive today?
2. Why will photovoltaic cells be less expensive when we can make many cells at the same time?
3. In your country, will many houses get all their electricity from photovoltaic cells in the future? Why or why not?

Computers Can Read

Introduction

    Blind people (people who cannot see) must learn a special method for reading. They must learn to read with their fingers. They learn a special alphabet called Braille. Braille letters consist of small raised dots. A blind person touches the dots with his fingers and "reads" the letters through his sense of touch.

The Braille alphabet is difficult to learn, and very few books are printed in Braille. Most newspapers and magazines are not printed in Braille, so blind people cannot read them. They must ask other people to read the newspapers and magazines for them.

This chapter is about a special computer, the Kurzweil Reading Machine. The Kurzwell machine can read books, magazines, newspapers, and many other printed materials. A blind person puts the material on the machine, and the machine reads the material aloud.

With the help of the Kurzweil Reading machine, blind people can now "read" more. They do not have to use Braille, and they do not have to ask other people to read for them.

Vocabulary Preparation

These diagrams will help you understand some of the words in this chapter.

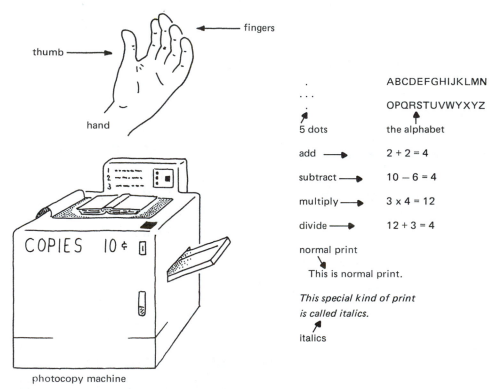

FIGURE 2-9   Vocabulary for "Computers Can Read"

Text

Computers Can Read

Computers have many uses today. Computers can solve difficult problems and control complex machines. Many people use small computers called calculators to add, subtract, multiply, and divide numbers quickly. Scientists use large computers to solve many problems at the same time. You can play games with computers, and some computers can help you learn languages. The Kurzweil Reading Machine is a special kind of computer. It can read books for blind people.

The Kurzweil machine consists of three components: a scanner, a computer, and a voice synthesizer. These three parts are like your eyes, your brain, and your voice (see Figure 2-10). The scanner is the "eye" of the machine. It

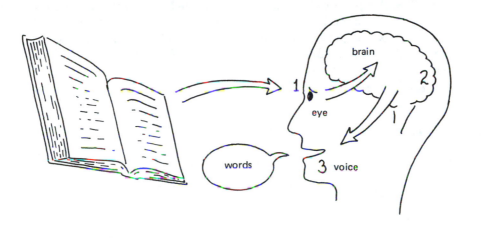

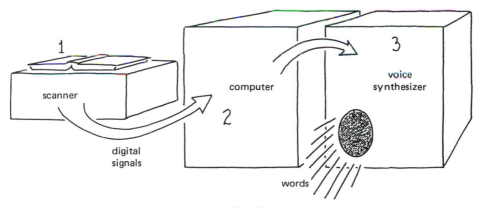

FIGURE 2-10   The Kurzweil Reading Machine

scans, or looks at, the words on the page of a book and changes them into digital signals. These digital signals then go to the computer, the "brain" of the machine. The computer analyzes the signals and recognizes the words. The computer sends information about the words to the voice synthesizer. The voice synthesizer makes the sounds of the words.

To use the machine, a blind person simply opens the book and puts it face down on the scanner (like a photocopy machine). The machine "reads" the words on the page. When one page is finished, the blind person turns the page and puts the book on the scanner again. The Kurzweil machine can read in a normal voice or in a special fast voice. It can read words with small letters, large letters, or italics.

Blind people like the Kurzweil machine because they can "read" anything with it: newspapers, magazines, books, even typed letters. Many libraries now have Kurzweil machines for blind people to use. The Kurzweil machine can also help sighted children learn to read.

Can the Kurzweil Reading Machine help you to read in English? The computer can analyze the grammar of sentences, and the voice synthesizer can make the sounds of the words. However, the machine cannot explain the meanings of the words. To use the machine, you must know the meanings of the words and sentences first.

Comprehension Questions

Directions: *Yes or no? Write "yes" or "no" in the space.*

1. Can the Kurzweil Reading Machine read books aloud?

   _____

2. Is the scanner the "brain" of the machine? _____

3. Does the voice synthesizer make the sounds of the words?

   _____

4. Does the scanner look like a photocopy machine?

   _____

5. Can the Kurzweil machine read in a special slow voice?

   _____

6. Do blind people like the Kurzweil machine? _____

7. Can the machine explain the meanings of words and sentences?

   _____

Directions: *Choose the best answer.*

1. What is the topic of the first paragraph of the text? (Note: See Unit 1 Paragraph Study for an explanation of "topic.")
   a. uses of computers
   b. calculators
   c. computer languages
   d. the Kurzweil Reading Machine

2. How many components does the Kurzweil machine have?
   a. one
   b. two
   c. three
   d. four

3. Which part of the machine is like your eyes?
   a. the computer
   b. the scanner
   c. the voice synthesizer
   d. the photocopy machine

4. How does the Kurzweil machine read?
   a. in a normal voice
   b. in a low voice
   c. in a fast voice
   d. in a normal voice or a fast voice

5. Why do blind people like the Kurzweil machine?
   a. They can "read" anything with it.
   b. It is a computer.
   c. It helps children learn to read.
   d. It can explain the meanings of words.

6. "These parts are like your eyes, your brain, and your *voice*." With your voice, you can _____.
   a. analyze sentences
   b. make digital signals
   c. recognize words
   d. make the sounds of words

7. "They can read *anything* with it." "Anything" means

   _____.

   a. some kinds of reading materials
   b. all kinds of reading materials
   c. no kinds of reading materials
   d. few kinds of reading materials

Directions: *What do you think? Write answers to these questions and discuss your answers with other students in your class.*

1. Why did the writer, or *author*, write this text?
   a. to show how computers work
   b. to make people buy the Kurzweil machine
   c. to show how blind people live
   d. to explain how the Kurzweil machine works

2. What kind of people did the author write this text for?
   a. computer scientists
   b. English students
   c. blind people
   d. people who work in libraries

3. How can the Kurzweil Reading Machine help students learn English as a second language?

4. In the future, will blind people learn the Braille alphabet?

UNIT 3 Reading Skills

WORD STUDY

1. Recognizing Restatements and Examples as Context Clues
2. Recognizing the Meaning of Suffixes and Prefixes
3. Choosing the Appropriate Dictionary Definition of a Word with Multiple Meanings

SENTENCE STUDY

1. Recognizing Pronoun References
2. Identifying Sentence Connectors
3. Recognizing Synonymous Sentence Elements

PARAGRAPH STUDY

1. Recognizing Appropriate Main Ideas for Paragraphs
2. Dividing Information According to Level of Generality

READING SPEED

1. Rapid Recognition of Identical Words and Phrases
2. Rapid Recognition of Paragraph Organization

Word Study

Recognizing Restatements and Examples as Context Clues

Sometimes a writer gives the meaning of a new word by explaining the meaning in another sentence.

EXAMPLE:

Professor Tracy belongs to several professional organizations. He is a member of the Teacher's Union, the Science Foundation, and the Association of Teachers of Science.

(The writer tells us that the meaning of "belongs to" in the first sentence is "to be a member of.")

Sometimes a writer gives the meaning of a new word by giving examples in other sentences.

EXAMPLE:

There are activities for foreign students every weekend. For example, the International Sports Club organizes soccer games every Saturday afternoon, the Foreign Student Association sponsors Saturday night dances every month, and the YMCA offers an international dinner every other Sunday night.

(The writer gives us examples of "activities": "soccer games," "Saturday night dances," and "international dinners." We can guess that "activities" are "things to do.")

Exercise 3–1

Directions: *Here are some groups of sentences. In each group of sentences, the writer gives the meaning of the underlined word. Sometimes the writer explains the meaning in another sentence, and sometimes the writer gives examples. Read the sentences and find the meaning of the underlined word. Then choose the* best *answer to the question. Please do* not *use your dictionary.*

1. The testing center will provide you with all the material you need. That is to say, you will not need to bring pencils, pens, paper, or dictionaries because the testing center will give you all of the things you need.

   What does provide mean?

   a. to bring something

   b. to give something to someone

    c. pencils, pens, paper, and dictionaries

    d. materials for taking a test

2. This test measures your ability to communicate. This means that it will tell us how well you can give information to other people and how well you can take information from people, books, or other sources.

    What do you do when you communicate?

    a. You give information to other people.

    b. You take information from different sources.

    c. You give and take information.

    d. You move from one place to another.

3. The library has many facilities to help people find information. These facilities include the library's books, newspapers, and magazines; the collections of films and tapes; the computer terminals; and the reference room where librarians can help you find many different kinds of information.

    What are the facilities of a library?

    a. things which help people find information

    b. people who use the library

    c. people who work in the library

    d. books which answer questions about the library

4. All over the world, people are learning English for different purposes. For example, some people are learning English because they need it for school. Some people are learning English for their work, and others want to learn English because it is spoken in so many different countries. The reason many people in business learn English is that it is used in international trade.

    What is a purpose?

    a. a way people do something

    b. a kind of learning

    c. a special kind of English

    d. a reason for doing something

5. I come from the United States, and my mother and father come from the United States, but my ancestors come from Europe. My mother's family came from England, and my father's family came from Germany.

    Who are my ancestors?

    a. my mother and father

    b. my mother's family and my father's family

    c. the United States

    d. England and Germany

6. Most car companies <u>guarantee</u> their new cars for one year. In other words, they promise that each new car will work well for one year, and they promise to fix the car if it does not work well during this time.

What does <u>guarantee</u> mean?

a. to promise that something will work well

b. to fix something which does not work

c. to work for one year

d. to make something new

7. Sally never gets lost because she has a good <u>sense</u> of direction. She does not need a map or a compass to help her because she always knows which way to go without thinking about it.

What does <u>sense</u> mean in these sentences?

a. intelligence

b. meaning

c. thinking

d. feeling

8. In this diagram, the first three figures have different <u>shapes</u>. Number 1 is a circle, 2 is a square, and 3 is a triangle.

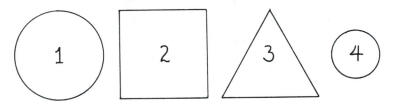

Which figures have the same <u>shape</u>?

a. 1 and 4

b. 1 and 3

c. 1, 2, and 3

d. none of the figures

9. Columbus <u>discovered</u> America in 1492. Before 1492, people in Europe did not know that America was on the other side of the Atlantic Ocean.

What does <u>discover</u> mean?

a. to go to a place

b. to make something new

c. to find something for the first time

d. to look for something

10. Success is the <u>result</u> of hard work. For instance, if you work hard at studying you will get good grades, and if you work hard at your job you will get more money or a better job.

Which one is not a <u>result</u> of hard work?

a. good grades

b. more money

c. studying

d. a better job

Recognizing the Meanings of Suffixes and Prefixes

Review of Suffixes: A *suffix* is a special ending for a word. A suffix can give information about the part of speech of a word. In Unit 1 Word Study we studied these noun and adjective suffixes:

	Suffix	Examples
NOUN SUFFIXES:	-ion	observation, information
	-er	reader, storyteller
	-or	collector, actor
	-ist	scientist, artist
	-ant	accountant, assistant
	-ent	student, independent
	-ian	technician, librarian
ADJECTIVE SUFFIXES:	-ic	scientific, public
	-al	digital, social
	-ous	dangerous, studious
	-ive	active, expensive

Here are three more suffixes. These suffixes also give information about the part of speech of a word.

NOUN SUFFIX:	-ity	activity, security
VERB SUFFIX:	-ate	communicate, activate
ADVERB SUFFIX:	-ly	carefully, regularly

Exercise 3-2

Directions: *Look at Table 3-1. Then complete the following sentences by finding the correct form of the underlined word in the table. Write the correct form of the missing word in the space. The first one is done for you.*

TABLE 3-1   Suffixes and Parts of Speech

Noun	Verb	Adjective	Adverb
information	inform	informative	informatively
communication	communicate	communicative	communicatively
extension	extend	extensive	extensively
activity	activate	active	actively
industry	industrialize	industrial	industrially
agriculture	—	agricultural	agriculturally
tradition	—	traditional	traditionally
facility	facilitate	—	—
translation	translate	—	—

1. When a book gives us a lot of <u>information</u>, we say that it is a

   very ____*informative*____ book.

      (adjective)

2. People can <u>communicate</u> by speaking, writing, making signs, or using

   pictures. The most common forms of _____ are

                              (noun)
   speaking and writing.

3. A <u>tradition</u> is an old way of doing something. Traditions do not

   change for a long time. _____, farmers used

                        (adverb)
   animals to do their work, for example; but today most modern farmers
   use machines to do their work.

4. <u>Activities</u> are things for people to do, and an _____

                                        (adjective)

   person is a person who is always doing something.

5. <u>Industries</u> are companies and factories which make things for people.

   Most developing countries want to _____ quickly

                              (verb)
   so that the people can have the things they want.

6. Our house is too small, so we are going to <u>extend</u> the house to make it

   bigger. We are going to build an _____ on the west

                              (noun)
   end of the house.

7. <u>Facilities</u> help us do our work more quickly and easily. We can do more work in a short time when we use facilities because they

   _____ the work.
   (verb)

8. <u>Agriculture</u> is very important to all countries. _____
   (adjective)

   activities include growing crops and raising animals.

9. When we <u>translate,</u> we change words from one language to another.

   Sometimes it is difficult to find a good _____.
   (noun)

10. Newspapers give <u>information</u> about the news of the day. They

    _____ people about what is happening in the world.
    (verb)

Suffixes that Add Meaning to a Word: Some suffixes give information about the part of speech of a word; other suffixes can change the meaning of a word. Here are four suffixes which can change the meaning of a word:

Suffix	Meaning	Examples
-ful	"full of"	successful ("full of success")
		careful ("full of care")
		useful ("full of uses")
-less	"without"	careless ("without care")
		useless ("without use")
		childless ("without children")
-able	"able to"	usable ("able to be used")
		understandable ("able to be understood")
-ness	"state of being"	happiness ("state of being happy")
		usefulness ("state of being useful")
		carelessness ("state of being careless")

Exercise 3-3

Directions: *Read each sentence and choose the* best *word for each space. Circle the letter of the best word. The first one is done for you.*

1. Dictionaries are very _____ for students because students can use them to find the meanings, the correct spelling, and the correct pronunciation of words.
   a. careless
   b. useful
   c. useless
   d. understandable

2. Some families are _____ because the husband and wife decide not to have children.
   a. childless
   b. useful
   c. happiness
   d. successful

3. A car is _____ if it will not start.
   a. careless
   b. usable
   c. careful
   d. useless

4. Prof. Jenkins' lectures are always _____ because he speaks clearly and explains everything very carefully.
   a. usable
   b. happiness
   c. usefulness
   d. understandable

5. Many mistakes are the result of _____.
   a. carelessness
   b. happiness
   c. successful
   d. careful

6. We cannot drink this polluted water, but it is _____ for washing.
   a. useless
   b. careless
   c. usable
   d. careful

7. A _____ student is a student who does well in all his or her classes.
   a. careless
   b. successful
   c. usable
   d. childless

8. A _____ driver obeys all of the rules.

   a. careless

   b. useful

   c. useless

   d. careful

Prefixes that Add Meaning to a Word: A suffix comes at the end of a word. On the other hand, a prefix comes at the beginning of a word. A prefix usually changes the meaning of a word.

Look at the following words. Some words have prefixes and some do not.

write	rewrite
historic	prehistoric
war	postwar
social	antisocial
spell	misspell
stop	nonstop
agree	disagree
usual	unusual
complete	incomplete
possible	impossible

The words "rewrite," "prehistoric," "postwar," "antisocial," "misspell," "nonstop," "disagree," "unusual," "incomplete," and "impossible" have prefixes. The prefixes are "re-," "pre-," "post-," "anti-," "mis-," "non-," "dis-," "un-," "in-," and "im-." Each prefix has a meaning.

Prefix	Meaning	Examples
re-	"again"	rewrite = "write again"
pre-	"before"	prehistoric = "before history"
post-	"after"	postwar = "after the war"
anti-	"against"	antisocial = "against society"
mis-	"wrongly"	misspell = "spell wrongly"
non-	"without"	nonstop = "without stops"
dis-	"not"	disagree = "not agree"
un-	"not"	unusual = "not usual"
in-	"not"	incomplete = "not complete"
im-	"not"	impossible = "not possible"

Exercise 3-4

Directions: *One word is missing in each of the following sentences. The missing words are this list:*

rewrite	misspell
prehistoric	nonstop
postwar	disagree
antisocial	unusual
incomplete	impossible

Find the best word for the sentence in the list and write it in the space. The first one is done for you.

1. Most birds can fly, so the ostrich is an _____*unusual*_____ bird because it cannot fly.

2. I made a lot of mistakes in my letter, so I will _____ the letter before I send it.

3. My homework is _____ because I did not have time to finish it.

4. If you fly _____ from New York, you will arrive in Los Angeles at 4:00 P.M.; if you stop in Chicago and Denver, you will arrive at 8:00 P.M.

5. People often _____ her name because there are many different ways to write it.

6. We know very little about life in _____ times because the people who lived in those times did not know how to write.

7. Some people think he is _____ because he likes to stay alone and does not like to talk to other people.

8. My friends think English is easy, but I _____ with them because learning English is very difficult for me.

Exercise 3-5

Directions: *Read the sentence and guess the meaning of the underlined word. Then write the meaning of the underlined word in the space. The first one is done for you.*

1. Many American marriages end in divorce, but most of these divorced people will find new husbands and wives and <u>remarry</u> after one or two years.

   remarry = _____*marry again*_____

2. Our library contains a large fiction collection (novels, short stories, and other books that tell a story); but most students use the library's <u>nonfiction</u> collection because these books contain important information for their studies.

   nonfiction = _____

3. Thousands of <u>antiwar</u> demonstrators marched to the capital city shouting "No more war!"

   antiwar = _____

4. If a teacher <u>misinforms</u> students, they will be confused because students always expect their teachers to give them the correct information.

   misinform = _____

5. Before industrialization, this was an agricultural society, but after years of being an industrial society it is becoming a <u>postindustrial</u> society.

   postindustrial = _____

6. When I was a child, I depended on my parents for food, clothing, and shelter; but now I am <u>independent</u> and must find these things for myself.

   independent = _____

7. In this book, vocabulary preparation is a <u>prereading</u> activity. First we study the vocabulary and then we read the text.

   prereading = _____

Choosing the Appropriate Dictionary Definition of a Word with Multiple Meanings

When you look for the meaning of a word in an English dictionary you often find many different *definitions,* or meanings, for the word. How can you choose the correct definition?

Most English words have more than one meaning, so the best way to choose the correct definition of a word is to look at the word in a sentence. Then try the different definitions of the word in the sentence. This will help you choose the best definition.

EXAMPLE:

Libraries *offer* many different services to people.

My dictionary gives five different definitions for the word "offer":

1. to present in worship (to *offer* prayers)
2. to present for acceptance (to *offer* help)

3. to suggest, propose (to *offer* a solution)

4. to show or give signs of (to *offer* resistance)

5. to bid (to *offer* a price)

When I try all five definitions in the sentence, I find that definition 2. (to present for acceptance) is the best definition for "offer" in this sentence.

Libraries "present for acceptance" many different services to people.

(*Note:* If you do not understand some of the words in the definitions, you can look them up in your English dictionary or your bilingual dictionary.)

Exercise 3-6

Directions: *Read each sentence and circle the letter of the best definition of the underlined word for that sentence. If you do not understand some of the words in the definitions, look them up in your English or bilingual dictionary.*

1. Libraries offer many different <u>services</u> to the people who use them.
   a. the occupation of a servant
   b. public employment
   c. work done for others
   d. a religious ceremony

2. Many American <u>marriages</u> end in divorce.
   a. state of being married
   b. a wedding
   c. a close union

3. When children grow up and get married, they <u>form</u> new families.
   a. to shape; fashion
   b. to train; instruct
   c. to develop (habits)
   d. to make up; constitute

4. Some libraries offer art <u>exhibits</u> for people who are interested in painting and sculpture.
   a. displays
   b. things exhibited
   c. objects used as evidence in court

5. Some people who do well in their fields find it difficult to <u>succeed</u> in language learning.
   a. to gain a purpose or reach an aim
   b. to do well, especially in gaining a position or popularity
   c. to follow after
   d. to be the next to take a position or <u>rank</u>

6. Libraries are offering more and more services for their <u>patrons</u>.
   a. protectors; benefactors
   b. people who sponsor some person, activity, etc.
   c. regular customers

7. There are many different kinds of families, but everyone has a <u>sense</u> of what a family is.
   a. meaning
   b. the five senses (hearing, seeing, touching, tasting, and smelling)
   c. power to understand and judge
   d. a feeling that is hard to describe exactly

8. I like to look at the <u>rows</u> of books in the library.
   a. numbers of people or things in a line
   b. lines of seats in a theater
   c. quarrels or fights

Sentence Study

Recognizing Pronoun Reference

Pronoun Reference within a Sentence: Writers often use pronouns when they do not want to use the same noun more than one time in a sentence. Here are some of the pronouns they use:

Personal Pronouns	Other Pronouns
I, me, my, mine	this, that
you, your, yours	these, those
he, him, his	some, others
she, her, hers	all, most, many, a few
it, its	few, none
they, them, their, theirs	

A pronoun always refers to a noun. Sometimes the pronoun takes the place of the noun.

EXAMPLES:

1. John told Marsha *he* wanted to talk to *her*.

   (*He* refers to John; *her* refers to Marsha.)
2. People go to libraries when *they* need information.

   (*They* refers to people.)

Sometimes the pronoun refers to part of the noun, or it shows that something belongs to the noun.

EXAMPLES:

1. *Some* students study in the library, and *others* study in *their* rooms.

   (*Some, others,* and *their* refer to "students." *Some* students = one group of students, *others* = a different group of students, and *their* rooms = the students' rooms.)
2. John has *his* friends and Marsha has *hers*.

   (*His* refers to John, and *hers* refers to Marsha. *His* friends = John's friends, and *hers* = Marsha's friends.)

Exercise 3-7

Directions: *Here are some sentences with pronouns. Read the sentences and circle the letter of the correct answer to each question about the pronouns. The first one is done for you.*

When social scientists study families, *they* find that *they* have different shapes and sizes.

1. The first *they* refers to _____.
   - (a.) social scientists
   - b. families
   - c. shapes
   - d. sizes
2. The second *they* refers to _____.
   - a. social scientists
   - b. families
   - c. shapes
   - d. sizes

When most people thing of libraries, *they* think of books.

3. In this sentence, *they* refers to _____.
   a. most people
   b. libraries
   c. books

There are as many different library services as there are types of people who use *them*.

4. *Them* refers to _____.
   a. there
   b. library services
   c. people

No matter whether *it* is young or old, large or small, traditional or modern, every family has a sense of what a family is.

5. *It* refers to _____.
   a. young or old
   b. large or small
   c. sense
   d. family

Music lovers can listen to recordings of *their* favorite musicians in the Music Library.

6. *Their* favorite musicians means the favorite musicians of

   _____.
   a. music lovers
   b. recordings
   c. the Music Library

Because *they* are all related, the members of an extended family are called relatives.

7. *They* refers to _____.
   a. extended families
   b. the members of an extended family
   c. people

Some families have long histories, while *others* know very little about *their* ancestors.

8. *Others* refers to _____.
   a. families
   b. histories
   c. ancestors

9. *Their* refers to _____.
   a. some families
   b. long histories
   c. other families

Successful language learners find people who speak the language and *they* ask these people to correct *them* when *they* make mistakes.

10. The first *they* refers to _____.
    a. successful language learners
    b. people who speak the language
    c. mistakes

11. The second *they* refers to _____.
    a. successful language learners
    b. people who speak the language
    c. mistakes

12. *Them* refers to _____.
    a. successful language learners
    b. people who speak the language
    c. mistakes

Pronoun Reference between Sentences: Sometimes writers use a pronoun in one sentence to refer to a noun in a different sentence.

EXAMPLE:

1. More and more libraries are offering special services for their patrons. *These* include entertainment facilities, community activities, and facilities for blind readers.

   (*These* refers to "special services.")

2. Some people think of a family as a mother, a father, and their children. *Others* include grandparents, uncles, aunts, and cousins.

   (*Others* refers to "people." *Others* = other people.)

Writers also often use the pronouns "you, your, yours" or "we, us, our, ours" to refer to the reader.

    EXAMPLE:

1. Perhaps *your* language learning has been less than successful. Then *you* might do well to try some of these techniques.

    (*Your* and *you* refer to the reader.)

2. Most of *us* know what a family is. However, *we* can learn more about families from social scientists.

    (*Us* and *we* refer to the reader and the writer.)

Exercise 3-8

Directions: *In these paragraphs, the pronouns are underlined and there is a space above each pronoun. Read the paragraph and find the noun to which each pronoun refers. Write the noun in the space above the pronoun. The first two are done for you.*

1.   (_____*learning a language*_____)

    "Learning a language is easy. Even a child can do it."
Most adults who are learning a second language would disagree with

    (_____*most adults*_____)

this statement. For them learning a language is a very difficult

    (_____)

task. They need hundreds of hours of study and practice, and

    (_____)

even this will not guarantee success for every adult learner.

2.   (_____)

In this chapter, we will discuss some of the ways in which people form

    (_____)

family groups. It will also include some information on the ways in

    (_____)

which they have changed over the years.

3. (_____)

Your local library is a good source of information and entertainment.

Most libraries have nonfiction collections of books about many different

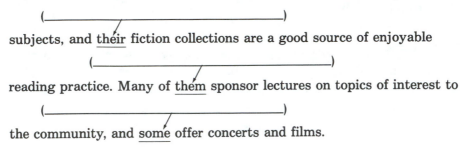

subjects, and their fiction collections are a good source of enjoyable

reading practice. Many of them sponsor lectures on topics of interest to

the community, and some offer concerts and films.

Identifying Sentence Connectors

Writers often use signal words like "and," "also," "but," and "however," to join sentences (see Unit 1 Sentence Study). These signal words give information about the two sentences. "And" and "also" tell the reader that the second sentence gives *more* information about the first sentence. "But" and "however" tell the reader that the second sentence gives *different* information from the first sentence.

Here are some more signal words that writers use to join sentences:

Signal Words	Meanings
and also moreover furthermore in addition	The second sentence gives *more* information about the first sentence.
but however on the other hand conversely yet although nevertheless while	The second sentence gives *different* information from the first sentence.

Signal Words	Meanings
so therefore consequently thus	The second sentence gives the *result* of the information in the first sentence.

Exercise 3–9

Directions: *Here are some sentences joined with signal words. Read each sentence and look for the signal word. Underline the signal word. Does the second sentence give* more *information about the first sentence,* different *information from the first sentence, or the* result *of the information in the first sentence? Write "more," "different," or "result" in the space. The first one is done for you.*

1. I enjoy reading the newspapers from my country, <u>although</u> they are always two or three weeks late.

   different

2. There are millions of books in our library; consequently, we use a special system to keep the books in order.

   _____

3. Some families have long histories while others know very little about their ancestors.

   _____

4. They are all related to each other, so the members of an extended family are called relatives.

   _____

5. The nuclear family is becoming smaller as parents want fewer children; furthermore, many nuclear families are "splitting up" as more and more parents get divorced.

   _____

6. Some people can learn languages more quickly than others, yet they do not seem to be more intelligent than others.

   _____

7. Some people who are successful in their fields cannot learn languages easily. Conversely, some successful language learners cannot do well in other fields.

---

8. Successful language learning is active learning. Therefore, successful language learners always look for chances to use the language.

---

9. Successful language learners want to learn with the new language; thus, they find it easy to practice using the language regularly.

---

10. Most libraries have a reference collection, a periodicals collection, a non-fiction collection, and a fiction collection. Moreover, many libraries have special collections, such as children's collections, music collections, and art collections.

Recognizing Synonymous Sentence Elements

It is not necessary to know the meaning of every word in a sentence. A good reader can often guess the meaning of a new word or group of words. The meaning of the sentence helps the reader guess.

EXAMPLE:

A library is a good source of information, but libraries provide entertainment *as well as* information.

What does *as well as* mean in this sentence?

    a. Entertainment is *the same* as information.

    b. Libraries provide *both* entertainment *and* information.

    c. Entertainment is *as good as* information.

    d. Entertainment is *better than* information.

(The correct answer is b.)

EXPLANATION:

The first part of the sentence says that libraries provide information. The second part of the sentence says that libraries provide entertainment, so we can guess that "entertainment *as well as* information" means "*both* entertainment *and* information."

Exercise 3–10

Directions: *Read the sentence and guess the meaning of the underlined word or group of words. Then check (✔) the word or words with the same meaning. The first one is done for you.*

1. When most people think of libraries, they think of books—<u>rows and rows</u> of books about many different subjects.

   _____ a. two rows

   __✔__ b. many rows

   _____ c. too many rows

2. Today, a library is <u>much more than just</u> a place where books are stored.

   _____ a. only this kind of place

   _____ b. more than this kind of place

   _____ c. more libraries are becoming this kind of place

3. Today <u>more and more</u> libraries are offering special services for their patrons.

   _____ a. more libraries are doing this now

   _____ b. most libraries do this now

   _____ c. all libraries do this now

4. There are many different types of families, but <u>no matter whether</u> it is young or old, large or small, traditional or modern, every family has a sense of what a family is.

   _____ a. the type of family is important

   _____ b. the type of family is not important

   _____ c. no families are like this

5. <u>With the change</u> from an agricultural society to an industrial society, many families move away from the family home to find work in the cities.

   _____ a. to make this change happen

   _____ b. before this change happens

   _____ c. when this change happens

6. "Learning a language is easy; <u>even a child</u> can do it."

   _____ a. only a child can do this

   _____ b. children as well as adults can do this

   _____ c. a child cannot do this

7. Successful language learners <u>do not seem to be any more intelligent</u> than unsuccessful language learners.

_____ a. they are as intelligent

_____ b. they are more intelligent

_____ c. they are less intelligent

8. <u>Instead of waiting</u> for an answer, successful language learners look for an answer.

_____ a. they do not wait

_____ b. they always wait

_____ c. they sometimes wait

Paragraph Study

Recognizing Appropriate Main Ideas for Paragraphs

Every paragraph has a *topic* (see Unit 1 Paragraph Study). All of the sentences in the paragraph are about the topic. The topic of a paragraph is like the subject of a sentence.

Each sentence in a paragraph says something about the topic. The *main idea* of a paragraph is one sentence that tells what *all* of the sentences say about the topic. Every paragraph has a main idea. It is like a summary of the information in the paragraph. To find the main idea of a paragraph, first find the topic of the paragraph. Then find what all of the sentences say about the topic.

EXAMPLE:

There are many ways to improve your vocabulary in English. One way is to read fiction (novels and stories) in English. Novels and stories often contain new words. It is not difficult to understand these new words because you can usually guess their meanings. The other words in the sentences will help you, and the story will also help you. An interesting story will help you understand the new words because the meanings of the new words are part of the meaning of the story.

First, what is the topic of the paragraph?

a. new words

b. ways to improve your vocabulary

c. novels and stories

d. one way to improve your vocabulary

(The correct answer is d. because all of the sentences in the paragraph are about *one* way to improve your vocabulary.)

Now, what do all of the sentences say about the topic?

a. There are many ways to improve your vocabulary.
b. One way to improve your vocabulary is to read fiction.
c. New words will help you to improve your vocabulary.
d. An interesting story will help you understand new words.

(The correct answer is b. because "one way to improve your vocabulary" is the topic, and all of the sentences say that one way to do this is "to read fiction"; so the *main idea* of the paragraph is: "One way to improve your vocabulary is to read fiction.")

Exercise 3–11

Directions: *Read the following paragraphs and answer the questions about the topics and main ideas of the paragraphs.*

PARAGRAPH 1

Do you want to know more about your family history? Maybe a geneologist can help you. A geneologist is specially trained to find information about family histories from many different sources. Some of this information comes from old records, such as birth certificates, marriage certificates, and death certificates. Often the geneologist finds information in old newspapers, tax records, or immigration records. It may even be necessary to visit distant towns and villages to collect information from the people who live there. Once the information is complete, the geneologist writes a geneology which describes the family's history.

1. What is the *topic* of this paragraph?
   a. families
   b. geneologists
   c. information about family histories
   d. writing a geneology

2. What is the *main idea* of this paragraph?
   a. A geneology describes a family's history.
   b. Geneologists look for information in different places.
   c. Geneologists can find information about family histories.
   d. Information about family histories comes from many different sources.

PARAGRAPH 2

Most children are excellent language learners. They can learn a second language quickly and easily. Most adults, on the other hand, find learning a second language difficult. They must study hard, and it usually takes them a long time to master the language. Adults usually try to learn a second language the same way they learn mathematics, science, history, or other subjects; but children learn a second language the same way they learned their first language. The child language learner has all the necessary skills to learn another language, but the adult language learner often has to relearn these skills in order to learn a second language.

3. What is the *topic* of this paragraph?
   a. language learning
   b. child language learners
   c. adult language learners
   d. child and adult language learners

4. What is the *main idea* of this paragraph?
   a. Children are excellent language learners.
   b. Adults find language learning difficult.
   c. Children are better language learners than adults.
   d. Children can learn more quickly and easily than adults.

PARAGRAPH 3

PLATO is my favorite teacher. He is very patient with me. He never gets tired or angry when I make too many mistakes. He always explains everything very carefully and makes sure that I answer every question correctly. When I need extra help after class, he is always in his "office"—even late at night. Not only does he teach me English, but he is also teaching me to type. But PLATO is not as friendly as my human teachers. He never smiles or laughs, and he doesn't ask about my family or what I plan to do next weekend. In fact, he doesn't talk at all. You see, PLATO is a computer, a special computer that teaches me English.

5. What is the *topic* of this paragraph?
   a. PLATO
   b. my favorite teacher
   c. English techers
   d. computers

6. What is the *main idea* of this paragraph?
   a. PLATO is my favorite teacher.

b. Computers are better than human teachers.

c. PLATO is a special computer that teaches English.

d. Human teachers are more friendly than computers.

PARAGRAPH 4

The government of India encourages married men and women to be sterilized so they cannot have more children. In China, families can be punished for having more than one child. Both of these countries have very large populations, and if the number of people continues to increase, there will not be enough food, houses, or jobs for the people. As a result, India, China, and other populous countries are following a family-planning policy—they want families to limit the number of children they will have. Teachers, doctors, and social workers are explaining to the people why they should have fewer children by using birth control methods such as contraception and sterilization.

7. What is the *topic* of this paragraph?
   a. India and China
   b. sterilization
   c. the governments of India and China
   d. family planning

8. What is the *main idea* of this paragraph?
   a. Some populous countries are following a family-planning policy.
   b. India and China have very large populations.
   c. The government of India encourages sterilization.
   d. In China, families can be punished for having more than one child.

PARAGRAPH 5

Before the introduction of the computer search, library research was a long and tedious task. Now, instead of spending long hours looking through the card catalog and periodical indexes for books and articles on your subject, you can have a computer do the looking for you. All you need to do is give your subject to the computer. This is not as easy as it sounds, however, because you must know exactly what your subject is, and you must express it in words the computer can understand. The computer then searches its memory for books and articles about your subject. It takes less than a second for the computer to complete its search. Finally, it prints a bibliography—a list of the authors and titles of the books and articles it has found—for your subject.

9. What is the topic of this paragraph?
   a. library research

    b. computer searches

    c. bibliographies

    d. looking for books and articles

10. What is the main idea of this paragraph?

    a. Library research is a long and tedious task.

    b. A bibliography is a list of authors and titles of book and articles.

    c. A computer can find books and articles for you.

    d. A computer search can save time in library research.

Dividing Information According to Level of Generality

Read the following paragraph about families. Then look at the following diagram.

There are basically two types of families: nuclear families and extended families. The nuclear family usually consists of two parents (mother and father) and their children. The mother and father form the nucleus, or center, of the nuclear family. The children stay in the nuclear family until they marry. Then they form new nuclear families.

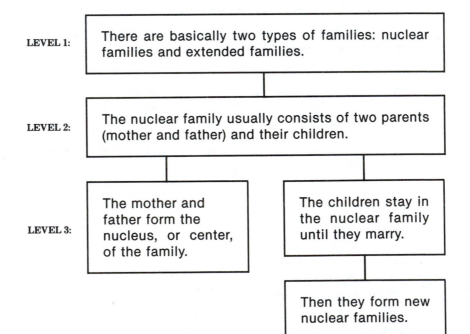

LEVEL 1: There are basically two types of families: nuclear families and extended families.

LEVEL 2: The nuclear family usually consists of two parents (mother and father) and their children.

LEVEL 3: The mother and father form the nucleus, or center, of the family.

The children stay in the nuclear family until they marry.

Then they form new nuclear families.

The writer organizes the information in this paragraph according to the level of generality. The diagram shows three levels of generality in the paragraph. We find the most general information at level 1: a general statement about families. At level 2, we find a more specific statement about one type of family, the nuclear family. The most specific information is at level 3. Here we find specific statements about the parents and the children in the nuclear family.

Exercise 3–12

Directions: *Read the following paragraphs and find the levels of generality of the information in each paragraph. Then complete the diagrams to show how the writer organized the information in each paragraph.*

PARAGRAPH 1

Libraries can be divided into two major groups: public libraries and academic libraries. Public libraries include state, county, and city libraries. A public library provides library services for all of the people in the community. An academic library, on the other hand, is generally a university library. It provides services for students, professors, and other members of the academic community. Because they are for all of the people, public libraries are a good source of books and magazines for entertainment. Most of the books and magazines in an academic library, however, are for research.

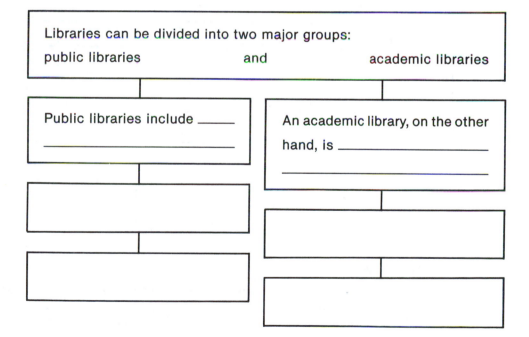

PARAGRAPH 2

Different language learners have different purposes for learning a new language. Some people learn a second language in order to learn about the culture of the people who speak that language. They may be interested in the history and the customs of these people, for example, or they may want to study the literature of the language. Other language learners want to travel to other countries. They need to know the languages of those countries so that they can talk to people and understand what they say. They want to make friends with the people they meet. Many people learn languages for professional reasons. These people want to learn more about their fields by studying in other countries or reading books and journals in different languages. They often need to use other languages in their work.

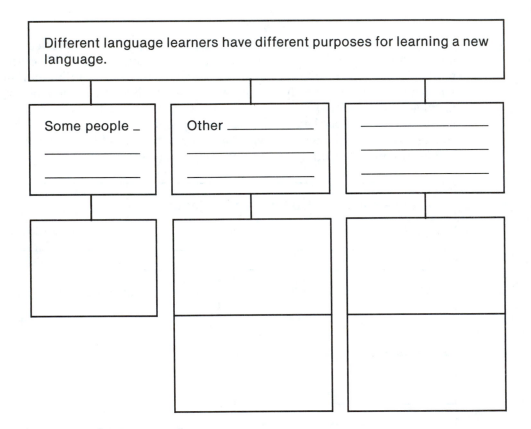

PARAGRAPH 3

To explain what I mean by a "typical American family," I will use my host family as an example. Mr. and Mrs. Smith have been married for twenty years. They have two children: a boy and a girl. Mr. Smith is an engineer with a well-known computer company. He enjoys his job and has been very successful at it. Mrs. Smith works part-time as a teacher and helps organize activities for the International Student Association in her spare time. Their son Dan is nineteen and a law student at a university in a different part of the country. He visits his family during Christmas and Easter vacations and works in a factory during the summer. Sarah, their daughter, is seventeen and will finish high school this year. She lives with her parents now but plans to move to an apartment when she graduates from high school. She wants to become an artist.

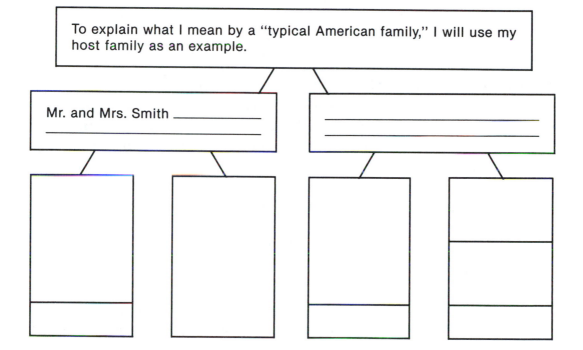

Reading Speed

Rapid Recognition of Identical Words and Phrases

Exercise 3–13

Directions: *Look at the first word. Then look at the other words on the same line. Find the first word and circle it. You may find the first word more than one time.*

EXAMPLE:

<u>marry</u>   many   merry   (marry)   many   (marry)   morning

1. (suggested time: 30 seconds)

<u>purpose</u>	propose	purpose	provide	propose	porpoise	purpose
<u>descended</u>	descended	decided	discarded	decided	descended	
<u>profile</u>	profit	profile	profile	profound	profane	profit
<u>nonfiction</u>	nonfunction	nonfiction	nonformal	nonfiction	nonfunction	
<u>belong</u>	belong	below	being	belong	balcony	below
<u>these</u>	there	their	these	there	this	their there
<u>whether</u>	whether	whither	weather	wither	whither	whether
<u>patron</u>	matron	patron	baton	patrol	baton	patron matron

2. (suggested time: 30 seconds)

<u>offer</u>	often	after	other	offer	often	after	other	often
<u>even</u>	ever	even	oven	ever	every	even	over	oven
<u>form</u>	farm	form	forum	from	form	forum	form	from
<u>facility</u>	facility	factory	faculty	factory	faculty	facility		
<u>service</u>	survive	service	severe	survive	severance	severe		
<u>shapes</u>	shades	shares	shaves	shapes	shares	shades	shapes	
<u>sense</u>	sense	since	science	sense	since	sense	scenes	

Exercise 3-14

Directions: *Look at the key phrase. Then look at the other phrases in the list. Find the key phrase and circle it. You may find the key phrase more than one time. Read as quickly as you can and try to finish in the suggested time.*

EXAMPLE:

Key phrase: <u>no matter whether</u>

no matter when

(no matter whether)

no matter what

not many which

(no matter whether)

(no matter whether)

no matter when

no matter which

to matter whether

(no matter whether)

How many times did you find the key phrase? ___4___

1. Key phrase: <u>as well as</u>   (suggested time: 30 seconds)

   as full as

   as well as

   as well is

   is well as

   as for as

   as much as

   as well as

   as many as

   as full as

   as far as

   as well as

   as much as

   as low as

How many times did you find the key phrase? _____

2. Key phrase: <u>special collections</u>   (suggested time: 20 seconds)

   special collections

   special collectors

   special services

   specific collections

   special collectors

   special collections

   special services

   service collections

specific collections

special collections

special corrections

specific corrections

special collectors

special corrections

How many times did you find the key phrase? _____

3. Key phrase: <u>a source of information</u>   (suggested time: 20 seconds)

a source of inspiration

a sort of inspiration

a source of information

a sort of information

a space for information

a source of information

a source of inspiration

a sort of investigation

a source of information

a sort of information

a scarcity of information

a source of inspiration

a source of information

How many times did you find the key phrase? _____

Exercise 3-15

Directions: *Look at the key phrase. Then look at the other phrases in the "paragraph." Find the key phrase and circle it. You may find the key phrase more than one time in the paragraph. Try to finish in the suggested time.*

EXAMPLE:

Key phrase: **reference collection**

(reference collection) reference librarian   reference correction

relevant collection   reference collector   relevant librarian

(reference collection) residence collection (reference collection)
relevance correction   reference collector

How many times did you find the key phrase? _____ *3* _____

1. Key phrase: **audio-visual material** (suggested time: 40 seconds)
   audio-lingual method   audio-visual method   audio-lingual
material   audio-visual material   audio-visual method   cardio-
vascular monitor   audio-lingual material   anti-venom medicine
audio-visual material   audio-visual material   audio-visual method
audio-lingual method   audio-lingual material

How many times did you find the key phrase? _____

2. Key phrase: **successful language learners** (suggested time: 40 seconds)
   successful language learning   successful language learners
resourceful language learners   successful language learning   second
language learners   computer language learners   successful language
learners   successive language learning   successfully learned
languages   second language learners   successive language learners

How many times did you find the key phrase? _____

3. Key phrase: **the extended family** (suggested time: 40 seconds)
   the extended family   the expanded family   the extended
frontier   three extended families   the extended family   the expensive family   the family expanded   the family expenses   the
expensive family   the expensive family   the expanded family   the
extended family   the extended formula   the extended formality
the intended family

How many times did you find the key phrase? _____

4. Key phrase: **the reference librarian** (suggested time: 40 seconds)
   the reference library   the reference collection   the reference
librarian   the research librarian   the reference collection   the
resident librarian   the research library   the reference library

the reference librarian   the resource librarian   the reference
librarian   the reluctant librarian   the reference collection
the reference librarian

How many times did you find the key phrase? _____

5. Key phrase: **learners with a purpose** (suggested time: 40 seconds)

learners without a purpose   learners with a purpose   learners
with a purpose   leaving with a purpose   learners without purpose
learners with a purpose   learners with no purpose   learning with
a purpose   learners with a purpose   leaving with a purpose
cleaners with a purpose   leavers with a purpose   learners with a
purpose

How many times did you find the key phrase? _____

Rapid Recognition of Paragraph Organization

Students often look for specific information in paragraphs when they are
studying. To find this information quickly, it is important to see how the information in the paragraph is divided. This exercise will help you do so.

Exercise 3-16

Directions: *Find the five paragraphs in Exercise 3-10. Read each paragraph
quickly to see how the information is divided, then answer the following
questions about the sentences in the paragraph. The first one is done for
you.*

PARAGRAPH 1

1. How many sentences are about what a geneologist does?
   __*4*__ (Sentences 1, 2, 3, and 7)

   EXPLANATION:
   Sentences 1 and 2 tell what a geneologist can do, sentence 3 is about a
   geneologist's training, and sentence 7 tells us what a geneologist writes.

2. How many sentences are about specific sources of information about
   family history? __*3*__ (sentences 4, 5, and 6)

EXPLANATION:

Sentence 4 is about getting information from old records, sentence 5 is about getting information from newspapers, tax records, and immigration records, and sentence 6 is about getting information from people in towns and villages.

PARAGRAPH 2

3. How many sentences are only about *child* language learners? _____

4. How many sentences are only about *adult* language learners? _____

5. How many sentences are about *both* adult and child language learners? _____

PARAGRAPH 3

6. How many sentences tell the *good* things about PLATO? _____

7. How many sentences tell *bad* things about PLATO? _____

PARAGRAPH 4

8. How many sentences are only about India? _____

9. How many sentences are only about China? _____

10. How many sentences are about both India and China? _____

PARAGRAPH 5

11. What are the three steps in the "computer search" process?

　　1) _____

　　2) _____

　　3) _____

UNIT 4 Reading Passages

FOR YOUR INFORMATION

1. Introduction
2. Vocabulary Preparation
3. Text
4. Comprehension Questions
5. Additional Reading

FAMILIES

1. Introduction
2. Vocabulary Preparation
3. Text
4. Comprehension Questions

A PROFILE OF THE SUCCESSFUL LANGUAGE LEARNER

1. Introduction
2. Vocabulary Preparation
3. Text
4. Comprehension Questions

For Your Information

Photo by Cheri Wilder

Introduction

When most people think of libraries, they think of books—rows and rows of books about many different subjects. All libraries have books, of course, but most modern libraries offer more than just books.

Most libraries have a reference collection, a periodicals collection, a non-fiction collection, and a fiction collection. Moreover, many libraries have special collections, such as children's collections, music collections, and art collections. More and more libraries are offering special services for their patrons, the people who use the libraries. These include entertainment facilities, community activities, and facilities for blind readers.

This chapter is about some of the unusual services which modern libraries provide. It will show that libraries today are much more than just places where books are stored.

Vocabulary Preparation

> **Directions:** *Read the sentences and* guess *the correct meanings of the underlined words. Then answer the questions. Please do* not *use your dictionary.*

1. At first I wanted to buy a new car, but I discovered that the prices of used cars were much lower.

   A used car is _____.

   a. a new car

   b. a broken car

   c. an older car

   d. a smaller car

2. Jerome wanted to read the book, but he did not want to buy it. Therefore, he checked the book out of the library to read it.

   A library is _____.

   a. a place that sells books

   b. a photocopy machine

   c. a kind of inexpensive book

   d. a place where people borrow books

3. Mr. and Mrs. Pond like classical music—Bach, Beethoven, Brahms, etc.—but their children like popular music. Seth likes to listen to disco and rock-and-roll tapes, while his sister likes to dance to Country and Western records.

   Which of the following is *not* a kind of music?

   a. records and tapes

   b. classical

   c. rock and roll

   d. popular

4. "What do you do for entertainment in a small town like this?" "Well, I go to the movies once a week. On weekends we sometimes drive to a nightclub in the city. During the week I usually stay home after work and read a book or watch television."

   Which of the following is *not* a kind of entertainment?

   a. the movies

   b. a night club

   c. television

   d. work

5. We have two governments: a <u>local</u> government and a national government. The <u>local</u> government makes laws only for the people in this small
part of the country. The national government makes laws for all the people in the country.

<u>Local</u> means _____.

a. for a small part of the country

b. for all the people in the country

c. only for the people

d. a government which makes laws

6. Dr. Simpson is <u>in a hurry</u>. His train is leaving in ten minutes. He jumps
off the bus and runs inside the train station. He pushes to the front of
the line and quickly buys his ticket. Then he runs down the platform to
get on the train. Suddenly he stops—he remembers that he has carelessly
left his suitcase on the bus!

<u>In a hurry</u> means _____.

a. forgetting something

b. being late for something

c. doing something quickly

d. being careless

7. "This is a <u>public</u> library," the librarian explained. "It belongs to all of the
people, not just a few. This means that anyone who wants to use the library can use it."

<u>Public</u> means _____.

a. not all people can use it

b. belonging to all people

c. having many uses

d. belonging to just a few

8. This year, Podunk University will <u>sponsor</u> a bicycle race. The University
will pay for the event, and it will be called the Podunk University Bicycle
Race.

To <u>sponsor</u> a race is to _____.

a. pay for the race in return for advertising

b. join a race and win it

c. pay money to join the race

d. pay money to win the race

9. Everyone enjoys listening to recordings of famous musicians, but listening to recordings is not the same as attending a live <u>concert</u>. In a concert,

you can watch the conductor as he directs the orchestra and see the performers making their music on stage.

A <u>concert</u> is a _____.

a. recording

b. play or drama

c. kind of classical music

d. live musical event

10. People are always making things, but when they make something beautiful, we call it <u>art</u>. We find <u>art</u> in painting, sculpture, music, dance, and literature; but buildings, gardens, furniture, and even machines can also show <u>art</u>.

Which of the following is *not* <u>art</u>?

a. a mountain

b. a beautiful building

c. a flower garden

d. a famous novel

11. Libraries contain both <u>fiction</u> and nonfiction books. For example, Sir Thomas More's book *Utopia*, a story about an unreal island where everything is perfect, would be in the <u>fiction</u> collection. On the other hand, a book which gives facts about a real island would be in the nonfiction collection.

A book in the <u>fiction</u> collection of a library will contain

_____.

a. true facts

b. a story which is unreal

c. information about islands

d. only perfect things

12. <u>Short stories</u> are a source of entertainment, not of information.

In which part of the library would you find <u>short stories</u>?

a. the small book collection

b. the children's collection

c. the fiction collection

d. the nonfiction collection

Directions: *Read the sentences and use your dictionary to answer the questions about the underlined words.*

1. Books are arranged in <u>rows</u> on the shelves of a library.

   What does <u>rows</u> mean in this sentence?

   a. trips in rowboats

   b. neat lines

   c. difficult lives

   d. quarrels

2. Most libraries have a <u>reference</u> collection.

   What do you think a <u>reference</u> collection contains?

   a. books with specific information about specific topics

   b. written information about a person's character

   c. bad comments about someone

   d. connections with other parts of the library

3. Before we had books, people <u>stored</u> information in the human memory, that part of the brain which remembers. Today, information can be <u>stored</u> in books or in the memory of a computer.

   What does <u>stored</u> mean in these sentences?

   a. sold in a shop

   b. filled with supplies

   c. a large amount of something

   d. kept to use in the future

4. Many libraries use computer <u>terminals</u> to get information that is <u>stored</u> in a computer far away.

   What is the meaning of <u>terminal</u> in this sentence?

   a. an electrical connection point

   b. a transportation station

   c. the end of a line

   d. the end of a period of time

5. Michelangelo was a painter and sculptor of the Italian Renaissance. He is best known for his paintings on the ceiling of the Sistine Chapel in Rome, and his most famous <u>sculpture</u> is the huge statue "David," which he carved from a single block of marble.

   Which word has almost the same meaning as <u>sculpture</u>?

   a. painting

   b. ceiling

   c. statue

   d. marble

6. Most libraries provide services for children, and many <u>offer</u> special services for blind people.

Which word has almost the same meaning as <u>offer</u>?

a. services

b. provide

c. special

d. blind

7. There is a difference between a university <u>catalog</u> and a card <u>catalog</u>. One gives information about courses of study; the other gives information about books in a library.

a. Which one gives information about courses of study? (Write your answer in the space.)

_____

b. Which one gives information about books in a library? (Write your answer in the space.)

_____

8. Nancy is writing a <u>research</u> paper about utopian communities. First she found some books about utopian communities in the library. Then she read some articles about utopian communities in old newspapers and magazines. Now she is writing about what she has learned.

<u>Research</u> means _____.

a. reading books

b. reading articles

c. writing about something

d. finding information about something

Text

For Your Information

Are you looking for a good book to read? Do you need information about universities in the United States? Do you want to know the correct price of a used car? Would you like to read newspapers and magazines from different countries? Do you need a quiet place to study? Did you answer "yes" to any of these questions? Then you should visit "the information place"—your local library.

A library is more than just a place where books are stored. A library is a source of information. That information may come from books (fiction, nonfiction, or reference books), from periodicals (newspapers, magazines, and journals), from audio-visual material (records, cassettes, microfilm, video tapes, etc.), or even from a computer terminal.

Students go to libraries to study and to write research papers. The periodicals room of a university library is where foreign students often find newspapers and magazines from their countries. In the reference room, they can find catalogs from many universities in the U.S. and other countries. If you are buying a used car, the reference librarian can show you the *Blue Book,* which lists the prices of new and used cars. People who need information in a hurry can telephone the reference librarian at many libraries.

There are as many different library services as there are types of people who use them. Children's libraries provide materials for young readers. They sometimes have story-tellers who read stories to groups of children, and a few have computers for the children to play with. Music lovers can listen to recordings of their favorite musicians in music libraries. Some libraries have painting and sculpture exhibits, and most libraries offer special services for blind people, such as books in Braille, "talking" books, and Kurzweil Reading Machines (see Unit 2, "Computer Can Read").

Libraries provide entertainment as well as information. Novels and short stories from a library's fiction collection are a good source of enjoyable reading practice. Public libraries often sponsor lectures on topics of interest to members of the community, and a few even offer concerts and films. No matter what your interests are, you will find that a library can be a great place to enjoy yourself while you learn.

Comprehension Questions

Directions: *Yes or no? Write "yes" or "no" in the space.*

1. Is a library just a place where books are stored? _____

2. Do most university libraries have newspapers and magazines from many countries in their periodicals room? _____

3. Do reference librarians sell used cars? _____

4. Will some reference librarians give information by telephone?

   _____

5. Do most children's libraries have computers for the children?

   _____

6. Can you listen to recordings in music libraries? _____

7. Does the fiction collection of a library contain novels and short stories?

   _____

8. Do all libraries offer lectures, concerts, and films? _____

Directions: *Choose the* best *answer.*

1. What is another name for a library?
   a. a bookstore
   b. the periodicals room
   c. a reference librarian
   d. the information place

2. Newspapers, magazines, and journals are called

   _____.

   a. reference books
   b. periodicals
   c. audio-visual materials
   d. catalogs

3. In the reference room of the library you can find

   _____.

   a. the fiction collection
   b. newspapers and magazines
   c. university catalogs
   d. materials for young readers

4. Which of the following is *not* an example of a library service?
   a. used cars
   b. art exhibits
   c. children's story-tellers
   d. Kurzweil Reading Machines

5. "A library can be a great place to enjoy yourself while you learn." This
   means you can _____ in a library.
   a. talk and laugh as much as you want
   b. find entertainment and information
   c. play with computers
   d. have a lot of room to work

Topics and Main Ideas: (*Note:* See Unit 3 Paragraph Study for an explanation of "main idea.")

1. What is the *topic* of the first paragraph in the text?
   a. information
   b. questions
   c. books
   d. your local library

2. What is the *main idea* of the second paragraph?
   a. A library is a place where books are stored.
   b. A library is a source of information.
   c. Information comes from books, periodicals, audio-visual material, and computer terminals.

3. What is the *main idea* of paragraph 3?
   a. Students go to libraries to study.
   b. Foreign students like to read newspapers and magazines.
   c. People can use libraries in many ways.
   d. People go to the periodicals room or the reference room.

4. What is the *topic* of paragraph 4?
   a. libraries
   b. library services
   c. children's libraries
   d. services for blind people

5. What is the *main idea* of the whole text? Choose the *best* answer.
   a. There are many kinds of libraries.
   b. A library is a place where books are stored.
   c. Libraries provide entertainment
   d. Libraries offer many different services.

Pronoun Reference

Directions: *Find these sentences in the text and answer the questions.*

1. Are <u>you</u> looking for a good book to read? (Paragraph 1)

   <u>You</u> in this sentence refers to _____.
   a. the person who is reading the text
   b. the person who wrote the text
   c. one of the writer's friends

2. That <u>information</u> may come from books, from periodicals, from audio-visual material, or even from a computer terminal. (Paragraph 2)

In this sentence, <u>that information</u> means _____.

   a. information in a library
   b. information in books and periodicals
   c. information from university sources
   d. information from computer terminals

3. In the reference room, <u>they</u> can find catalogs from many universities in the U.S. and other countries. (Paragraph 3)

<u>They</u> refers to _____.

   a. libraries
   b. catalogs
   c. universities
   d. students

4. <u>They</u> sometimes have story-tellers who read stories to groups of children, and <u>a few</u> have computers for the children to play with. (Paragraph 4)

In this sentence, <u>they</u> refers to _____.

   a. young readers
   b. children's libraries
   c. story-tellers
   d. groups of children

<u>A few</u> means a few of the _____.

   a. story-tellers
   b. children
   c. children's libraries
   d. computers

Additional Reading

Manhungu is sitting at a long table reading *Jeune Afrique*, a French-language magazine he used to read at home in Zaire. His friend Mohammad is sitting beside him reading a newspaper from his country, Kuwait. On the other side of the room, Mercedes is standing in front of a photocopy machine. She is making copies of an article from *Business Week*.

These students are in the periodicals room, the magazine and newspaper section of the university library. "At home, I would buy *Jeune Afrique* every week," Mahungu says, "but I can't buy it here in Tennessee. Then a friend told me I could find it here in the library." Mohammad comes to the periodicals room between classes to read the Arabic newspapers. "Although they are always two or three weeks late, I enjoy reading them." Mercedes says she needs the magazines and journals in the periodicals room for her research because "it's the only way I can find the up-to-date information I need."

Directions: *Choose the* best *answer.*

1. Why does Mahungu read *Jeune Afrique* in the periodicals room?
   a. He needs it for his research.
   b. He cannot buy it in Tennessee.
   c. He could not read it in Zaire.
   d. He can only buy it in this library.

2. Why is Mercedes standing in front of the photocopy machine?
   a. She is making copies of an article.
   b. There is no room for her at the long table.
   c. She is on the other side of the room.
   d. There is up-to-date information in the machine.

3. Where does Mohammad go between classes?
   a. Kuwait
   b. the university
   c. Arabic newspapers
   d. the periodicals room

4. "Although they are always two or three weeks late, I enjoy reading them." Who said this?
   a. Mahungu
   b. Mohammad
   c. Mercedes
   d. the author

5. "It's the only way I can find the up-to-date information I need." Who said this?
   a. Mahungu
   b. Mohammad
   c. Mercedes
   d. the author

Directions: *What do you think? Write answers for these questions. Discuss your answers with other students in your class.*

1. What problem does Mohammad mention about the Arabic newspapers in the periodicals room? Why do you think this problem exists?

2. What does Mercedes say about the magazines and journals in the periodicals room? Why do you think this is true?

3. Why is Mercedes making photocopies of the *Business Week* article instead of taking the magazine home with her?

Finding a Needle in a Haystack

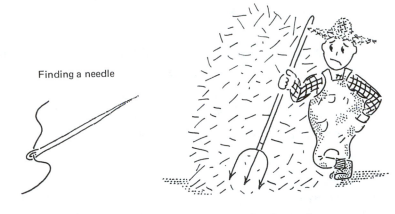

Finding a needle

In a haystack

  The Library of Congress, the largest library in the United States, contains about eighteen million books. Harvard University has the largest academic library with more than nine million volumes. The largest public library is the Chicago Public Library with nearly six million volumes, followed by the New York Public Library with 5.5 million. Consequently, finding a book in one of these libraries must be like finding a needle in a haystack!

  Librarians use a special system to make the job of finding books easier. To keep the books in order, librarians give a number to every book in the library, and books are arranged on the shelves according to these numbers. In order to find the number of a book, you must look in the card catalog. The card catalog is a special file of cards with information about the books in the library. Each book has three cards in the card catalog: a title card, an author card, and a subject card. These cards are arranged in the card catalog in alphabetical order. If you know the title of the book you are looking for, look for the title card. If you only know the author, look for the author card. If you are looking for a book about a particular subject, look for the subject card. When you find the card of the book you want, copy the number of the book. Then you can find the book easily.

Directions: *Choose the best answer.*

1. What is the topic of this reading?
   a. the largest library in the U.S.
   b. a special system for numbering books
   c. finding books in a library
   d. finding a needle in a haystack

2. The largest library in the United States is the _____.
   a. Library of Congress
   b. Harvard University Library
   c. Chicago Public Library
   d. New York Public Library

3. The largest academic library in the U.S. is the _____.
   a. Library of Congress
   b. Harvard University Library
   c. Chicago Public Library
   d. New York Public Library

4. How do librarians keep library books in order?
   a. They arrange the books in alphabetical order.
   b. They put the books into a card catalog.
   c. They give a number to each book.
   d. They put the books on the shelves.

5. The card catalog is a _____.
   a. special file of cards
   b. kind of library
   c. place to keep books
   d. special number system

6. If you know the title of a book, how can you find it quickly and easily?
   a. Look on the shelves of the Library.
   b. Look for the subject card in the card catalog.

   c. Find the author's name and look for the author card.

   d. find the title card and copy the number of the book.

Directions: *This is an author card from a card catalog. Answer the following questions by finding the information on the card. Write your answers in the spaces.*

382.24	Ramsay, James W. 1948–
R21	Basic Skills for Academic Reading. Englewood Cliffs, N.J.: Prentice-Hall (1986.) ix, 225 pp. illus. 25 cm.

1. What is the number of the book? _____

2. Who is the author of the book? _____

3. What is the title of the book? _____

   _____

4. Where was the book published? _____

5. When was the book published? _____

Directions: *What do you think? Write answers to the following questions. Discuss your answers with other students in your class.*

1. About how many cards would you expect there to be in the card catalog of the Library of Congress?

2. Imagine that you are looking for a book in the Harvard University Library. The book is about appropriate technology, it is by a man named Schumacher, and the title of the book is *Small Is Beautiful.* Which way do you think would be the *fastest* way to find the number of the book? Why?

   a. Look for the author card in the card catalog.

   b. Look for the subject card in the card catalog.

   c. Look for the title card in the card catalog.

   d. Look for the book on the shelves of the library.

Families

Introduction

"Family"—the word has different meanings for different people, and even the dictionary gives us several definitions: "a group of people related by blood or marriage," "two adults and their children," "all those people descended from a common ancestor," "a household," and so on. Some people think of a family as a mother, a father, and their children; others include grandparents, aunts, uncles, and cousins. For some of us, family means the group of relatives living far away from home. For others, having a family simply means having children. Some families have long histories, while others know very little about their ancestors. No matter if it is young or old, large or small, traditional or modern, every family has a sense of what a family is. It is that feeling of belonging, of love and security that comes from living together, helping and sharing.

When social scientists study families, they find that they have different shapes and sizes. This chapter is about some of the different types of families and how these families change as society changes.

Vocabulary Preparation

Directions: *Read the sentences and find the meanings of the underlined words in the sentences. Write the meanings of the words in the spaces. Please do not use your dictionary. The first one is done for you.*

1. John and Marsha were deeply in love when they got married, but later their marriage ended in <u>divorce</u> when they discovered that they no longer loved each other.

   divorce: _____*end of a marriage*_____

2. Acme Transport trucks bring <u>agricultural</u> products from the farms to people in the city, and they bring <u>industrial</u> products from the factories to the farmers.

   agricultural: _____

   industrial: _____

3. When I was a child, my parents provided food, clothing, and shelter for me. Now that I am an <u>adult</u>, I must provide these things for myself and my family.

   adult: _____

4. She is a <u>member</u> of three clubs. She belongs to the Chess Club, the Drama Club, and the Music Society.

   member: _____

5. Our <u>traditional</u> methods of farming were good in the old days when we had only a few people to feed, but now we need modern methods of farming to produce enough food for all our people.

   traditional: _____

6. There are more people in this <u>area</u> than in any other part of the country.

   area: _____

7. Many people like the <u>security</u> of a large group. Being with many other people gives them a feeling of being safe from danger.

   security: _____

8. Alex Haley did years of research for his book *Roots*. He wanted to find out where his <u>ancestors</u> came from, and after years of looking he found that some members of his family from the past came from the Gambia in West Africa.

   ancestors: _____

Directions: *Read the sentences and use your dictionary to answer the questions about the underlined words.*

1. When he checked his family history, he found that he was <u>descended</u> from Napoleon.

   This means that Napoleon _____.
   a. fell down
   b. was lower than him
   c. was his ancestor
   d. attacked his family

2. A British physicist named Rutherford was the first person to <u>split</u> the atom. This was the first step in developing nuclear power.

What did Rutherford do to the atom?

   a. He divided it into equal shares.

   b. He broke it into parts.

   c. He made it disappear.

   d. He made a bomb with it.

3. Although Gerald Ford and Henry Ford share a <u>common</u> name, they are not from the same family.

   In this sentence, <u>common</u> means _____.

   a. usual

   b. ordinary

   c. belonging to the public

   d. belonging to both people

4. President Franklin Delano Roosevelt was <u>related</u> to President Teddy Roosevelt. They were cousins.

   In this sentence, <u>related</u> means _____.

   a. of the same family

   b. told

   c. friendly

   d. connected in meaning

Text

Families

There are basically two types of families: *nuclear familes* and *extended families*. The nuclear family usually consists of two parents (mother and father) and their children. The mother and father form the nucleus, or center, of the nuclear family. The children stay in the nuclear family until they grow up and marry. Then they form new nuclear families (see Figure 4–1).

The extended family is very large. There are often many nuclear families in one extended family. An extended family includes children, parents, grandparents, uncles, aunts, and cousins. The members of an extended family are related by blood (grandparents, parents, children, brothers, sisters, etc.) or by marriage (husbands, wives, mothers-in-law, etc.). They are all related, so the members of an extended family are called relatives. Figure 4–2 shows some of the relatives in my extended family.

Traditionally, all the members of an extended family lived in the same

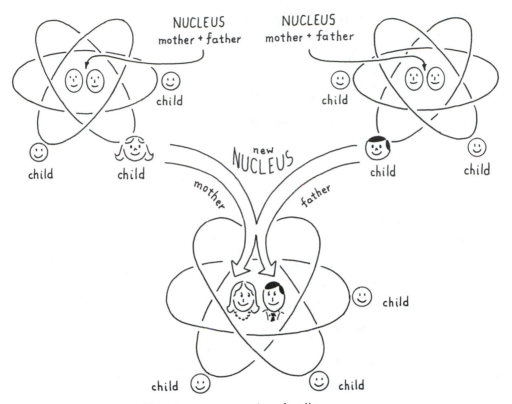

FIGURE 4-1　Forming a new nuclear family

area. However, with the change from an agricultural to an industrial society, many nuclear families moved away from the family home in order to find work. In industrial societies today, the members of most nuclear families live together, but most extended families do not live together. Therefore we can say that the nuclear family becomes more important than the extended family as the society industrializes.

In post-industrial societies like the United States, even the nuclear family is changing. The nuclear family is becoming smaller as parents want fewer children, and the number of childless families is increasing. Traditionally, the father of a nuclear family earned money for the family while the mother cared for the house and the children. Today, more than 50% of the nuclear families in the United States are *two-earner families*—both the father and the mother earn money for the family—and in a few families the mother earns the money while the father takes care of the house and the children. Many nuclear families are also "splitting up"—more and more parents are getting divorced.

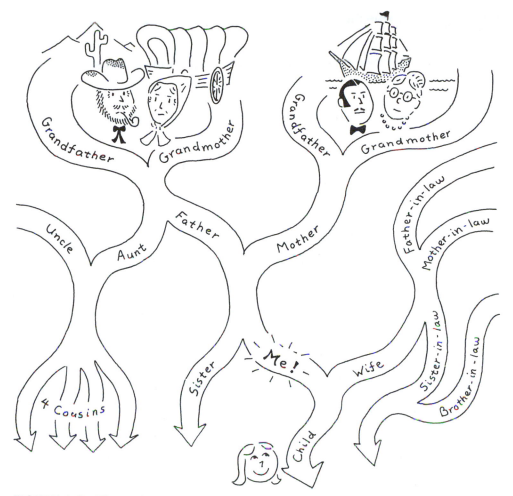

FIGURE 4–2   The author's extended family

What will be the result of this "splitting" of the nuclear family? Social scientists now talk of two new family forms: the *single-parent family* and the *remarried family*. In 1978, almost 20% of all American families were single-parent families, and in 85% of these families the single parent was the mother. Most single parents find it very difficult to take care of a family alone, so they soon marry again and form remarried families. As social scientists study these two new family forms, they will be able to tell us more about the future of the nuclear family in the post-industrial age.

Comprehension Questions

Directions: *Yes or no? Write "yes" or "no" in the space.*

1. Is the nuclear family larger than the extended family? _____

2. Do children form new nuclear families when they grow up and marry?

   _____

3. Are all the members of an extended family related by blood?

   _____

4. In the industrial societies, do the members of most extended families
   live together? _____

5. Traditionally, do both the mother and the father earn money for the
   nuclear family? _____

6. Are single-parent families the result of the splitting of nuclear families?

   _____

7. Are most American families single-parent families? _____

8. When divorced parents marry again, do they form remarried families?

   _____

Directions: *Find the answers to these questions in the text. Write the answers in the spaces.*

1. What are the two basic types of families?

   _____

   _____

2. What are the members of an extended family called? (one word)

   _____

3. What are the two new family forms that social scientists now talk of?

   _____

   _____

4. How many nuclear families in the United States are two-earner families?

_____

5. How many American families were single-parent families in 1978?

_____

6. In 1978, how many of the single-parent families in the United States included fathers? _____

Interpreting Diagrams: The diagram in Figure 4–2 is called a "family tree." It shows some of the relatives in the author's extended family.

Directions: *Find the answers to these questions in Figure 4–2.*

1. How many children do the author and his wife have?

_____

2. Is the author's sister married? _____

3. How many cousins does the author have? _____

4. How many children do the author's sister-in-law and brother-in-law have?

_____

5. How many brothers and sisters does the author's mother have?

_____

6. Is the author's uncle related to him by blood or marriage?

_____

Directions: *What do you think? Write answers to these questions. Discuss your answers with other students in your class.*

1. In your country, which is more important: the nuclear family or the extended family? Why?

2. In your country, do many nuclear families "split up"? Do you think more nuclear families will split up in the future? Why or why not?

3. What do you think will happen to the nuclear family in post-industrial societies like the United States in the future? Why do you think this will happen?

A Profile of the Successful Language Learner

Photo by Cheri Wilder

Introduction

"Learning a language is easy. Even a child can do it!"

Most adults who are learning a second language would disagree with this statement. For them, learning a language is a very difficult task. They need hundreds of hours of study and practice, and even this will not guarantee success for every adult language learner.

Language learning is difficult from other kinds of learning. Some people who are very intelligent and successful in their fields find it difficult to succeed in language learning. Conversely, some people who are successful language learners find it difficult to succeed in other fields.

Language teachers often offer advice to language learners: "Read as much as you can in the new language." "Practice speaking the language every day." "Live with people who speak the language." "Don't translate—try to think in the new language." "Learn as a child would learn; play with the language."

But what does a successful language learner do? Language learning research shows that successful language learners are similar in many ways. This chapter outlines the results of recent research on successful language learners and shows how you can become a more successful language learner.

Vocabulary Preparation

Directions: *Read the sentences and find the meanings of the underlined words* in the sentences. *Write the meanings of the words in the spaces. Please do* not *use your dictionary. The first one is done for you.*

1. Elroy finds learning Russian a difficult task. In fact, he thinks it is the most difficult piece of work he has done in his life.

   task: ___*a piece of work*___

2. The TOEFL Night School guarantees success in the TOEFL exam for all of its students. It promises that all students who take the course will get good results in the TOEFL exam.

   guarantee: _____

3. A knack for fixing cars is not something you can learn from books. It is a special skill, and it can only be learned from experience.

   knack: _____

4. Scientists have discovered a new technique for making batteries. This new method is much faster and less expensive than the old method for making batteries.

   technique: _____

5. The price of home computers will probably go down in the next five years. The price will almost certainly go down as computer factories find better ways to make these computers.

   probably: _____

6. She is a very active person. She is always busy doing something.

   active: _____

7. When you translate these words, be careful not to change the meaning of the words as you change them from one language to the other.

   translate: _____

8. The president will accept a few changes in the government, but he will not agree to have a complete change of government.

   accept: _____

9. I do not have enough time to tell you everything about my new book, but I can <u>outline</u> some of the main points for you.

   outline: _____

10. The text is called "A <u>Profile</u> of the Successful Language Learner" because it does not give a complete picture of the successful language learner. Instead, it gives a brief description of the successful language learner.

    profile: _____

Directions: *Read the sentences and* guess *the meanings of the underlined words. Then answer the questions. Again, please do* not *use your dictionary.*

1. Each student must find some information about his or her <u>field</u> in the library. Mercedes is looking for a book about business administration, Mahungu is looking for an article about statistics, and Mohammad is looking for information about computer science.

   Which of the following is *not* a <u>field</u>?

   a. business administation

   b. statistics

   c. a book

   d. computer science

2. People offer different <u>advice</u> about buying a used car. Some say, "Never buy a used car!" Others say that used cars are better than new cars. Some people advise used car buyers to buy only from a large company; others say that you will pay too much if you buy from a large company. Most people say that you should show the car to a good mechanic before you buy it. A few suggest that you take the car to two or three mechanics.

   Which of the following is *not* an example of <u>advice</u> about buying a used car?

   a. buy only from a large company

   b. pay too much

   c. show the car to a good mechanic

   d. never buy a used car

3. Inspector Clouseau was ready to solve the murder. "I find many <u>clues</u> here," he said, "but only one <u>clue</u> gives me the answer. The killer used a small knife to kill Mrs. Jones. The window was open for the killer to escape. The killer did not take the money from Mrs. Jones' purse. But the most important <u>clue</u> is this piece of blond hair in Mrs. Jones' hand. The only person in this house with blond hair is Olga the maid. She is the killer!"

Which of the following is not a clue?

a. the murder

b. the open window

c. the money in Mrs. Jones' purse

d. the piece of blond hair

Directions: *Read the sentences and use your dictionary to answer the questions about the underlined words.*

1. For many years, Nelson tried to master the game of chess.

   In this sentence, "master" means _____.

   a. a man in control of people or animals

   b. to teach something

   c. to become an expert

   d. a young boy

2. In romance languages (languages that come from Latin), words in a sentence generally follow the SVO pattern.

   In this sentence, "pattern" means _____.

   a. a regular repeated arrangement

   b. a shape used as a guide for making something

   c. to copy someone

   d. from Latin

3. A social scientist must learn how to work with inexact information.

   When I looked up the word "inexact" in my dictionary, I found that it means "not exact." But what does "exact" mean?

   a. to demand by force

   b. to make necessary

   c. correct and without mistakes

   d. very

4. The Host Family Program gives foreign students a chance to learn more about American family life.

   What does "chance" mean in this sentence?

   a. good or bad fortune

   b. accidental

   c. risk

   d. opportunity

Text

A Profile of the Successful Language Learner

Some people seem to have a knack for learning languages. They can pick up new vocabulary, master rules or grammar, and learn to write in the new language more quickly than others. They do not seem to be any more intelligent than others, so what makes language learning so much easier for them? Perhaps if we take a close look at these successful language learners we may discover a few of the techniques which make language learning easier for them.

First of all, successful language learners are independent learners. They do not depend on the book or the teacher; they discover their own way to learn the language. Instead of waiting for the teacher to explain, they try to find the patterns and the rules for themselves. They are good guessers who look for clues and form their own conclusions. When they guess wrong, they guess again. They try to learn from their mistakes.

Successful language learning is active learning. Therefore, successful learners do not wait for a chance to use the language; they *look* for such a chance. They find people who speak the language and they ask these people to correct them when they make a mistake. They will try anything to communicate. They are not afraid to repeat what they hear or to say strange things; they are willing to make mistakes and try again. When communication is difficult, they can accept information that is inexact or incomplete. It is more important for them to learn to think in the language than to know the meaning of every word.

Finally, successful language learners are learners with a purpose. They want to learn the language because they are interested in the language and the people who speak it. It is necessary for them to learn the language in order to communicate with these people and to learn from them. They find it easy to practice using the language regularly because they want to learn with it.

What kind of language learner are you? If you are a successful language learner, you have probably been learning independently, actively, and purposefully. On the other hand, if your language learning has been less than successful, you might do well to try some of the techniques outlined above.

Comprehension Questions

Directions: *Yes or No? Write "yes" or "no" in the space.*

1. Are successful language learners more intelligent than other language learners? _____

2. Do successful language learners depend on their books and teachers?

_____

3. Do successful language learners try to learn from their mistakes?

   _____

4. Do active language learners look for chances to use the language?

   _____

5. When communication is difficult, do successful language learners try to understand the meaning of every word? _____

6. Do successful language learners want to learn from people who speak the language? _____

7. Is it easy to practice a language when you want to learn with the language? _____

Directions: *Choose the* best *answer.*

1. What makes language learning easier for some people than for others, according to this text?
   a. Some people learn grammar more quickly than others.
   b. Successful language learners use special techniques.
   c. Some people have good teachers and good books.
   d. Successful language learners are more intelligent than others.

2. How do successful language learners learn languages?
   a. They learn independently, actively, and purposefully.
   b. They learn special techniques from their teachers.
   c. They learn the rules and patterns of the language from books.
   d. They learn to think about the meaning of every new word.

3. Why do successful language learners find it easy to practice using the language regularly?
   a. They find it easy to communicate.
   b. They look for inexact information.
   c. They want to teach the language to others.
   d. They want to learn from people who speak the language.

4. "If your language learning has been less than successful, you might do well to try some of the techniques outlined above." What does this sentence mean?
   a. Unsuccessful language learners should try the techniques of successful language learners.

b. Less successful language learners try to use successful language learning techniques.

c. Language learning is less successful if you use these techniques.

d. Less successful language learning is the result of using these techniques.

5. Why did the author write this text?

a. To teach people to speak English.

b. To explain why language learning is difficult.

c. To compare language learning with other types of learning.

d. To encourage language learners to use these techniques.

Directions: *The following sentences are incomplete. Choose the answer that best completes the sentence.* (Note: *See Unit 3 Paragraph Study for an explanation of "main idea."*)

1. The *main idea* of paragraph 2 is that successful language learners are

———————————————.

a. independent learners

b. good guessers

c. people who look for clues

d. people who learn from their mistakes

2. The *main idea* of paragraph 3 is that successful language learners

———————————————.

a. look for a chance to use the language

b. can accept inexact information

c. are not afraid to make mistakes

d. are active learners

3. The *main idea* of paragraph 4 is that successful language learners

———————————————.

a. find it easy to practice

b. communicate with other people

c. have a purpose for learning the language

d. have an interest in the people who speak the language

4. Independent learners discover their own way to learn instead of

   _____.

   a. depending on the book or the teacher
   b. picking up new vocabulary
   c. trying to learn from their mistakes
   d. finding patterns and rules for themselves

5. Active language learners _____ a chance to use the language.

   a. wait for
   b. look for
   c. are afraid of
   d. cannot accept

Directions: *What do you think? Write answers to the following questions. Discuss your answers with other students in your class.*

1. Is language learning more difficult than other kinds of learning? Why or why not?

2. Which is more important for successful language learning: language *learning* techniques or language *teaching* techniques? Why?

3. Do you think every person can learn to be a successful language learner? Why or why not?

UNIT 5 Reading Skills

WORD STUDY

1. Identifying Synonyms and Antonyms in Context
2. Recognizing Prefixes with Opposite Meanings
3. Identifying the Part of Speech of a Word in Context to Select the Appropriate Dictionary Definition

SENTENCE STUDY

1. Identifying Modifying Clauses and Phrases
2. Recognizing Synonymous Sentences

PARAGRAPH STUDY

1. Identifying Topic Sentences
2. Dividing Information According to Time, Place, and Causal Relationships

READING SPEED

1. Rapid Recognition of Identical Words and Phrases
2. Rapid Recognition of Synonyms
3. Recognition of Synonyms in Context

Word Study

Identifying Synonyms and Antonyms in Context

Synonyms and Antonyms: Sometimes two different words have the same meaning. Words that have the same meaning are called *synonyms*. For example, the words "large" and "big" are synonyms because they have the same meaning.

Sometimes two words have opposite meanings. Words that have opposite meanings are called *antonyms*. For example, the words "day" and "night" are antonyms because "day" is the opposite of "night."

Exercise 5-1

Directions: *Look at these pairs of words. Some of the words are synonyms: they have the same meaning. Some of the words are antonyms: they have opposite meanings. If the two words have the same meaning write "S" in the space. If the two words have the opposite meaning write "O" in the space. The first two are done for you.*

1. question answer _____O_____	11. few many _____
2. large big _____S_____	12. long short _____
3. rich poor _____	13. consent agree _____
4. huge large _____	14. cheap expensive _____
5. top bottom _____	15. strong powerful _____
6. sell buy _____	16. employ hire _____
7. certain sure _____	17. low high _____
8. war peace _____	18. funny amusing _____
9. enjoy like _____	19. locate find _____
10. always never _____	20. forget remember _____

Synonyms in Context: Sometimes a writer gives the meaning of a new word by using a synonym in another sentence. In these sentences, the writer uses a synonym of the word "law."

Sir Isaac Newton discovered the law of gravity. This rule tells us why things fall to the ground.

law = *rule*

EXPLANATION:

The word "this" in the second sentence tell us that "this rule" is the same as something in the first sentence. The first sentence tells us that Sir Isaac Newton discovered something, so we can guess that "this rule" is the same as "the law of gravity."

> Sir Isaac Newton discovered *the law of gravity.* (This rule) tells us why things fall to the ground.

The first sentence tells us that Newton discovered a law, and "of gravity" tells us what kind of law he discovered. If "this rule" has the same meaning as "the law of gravity," then we can guess that "rule" has the same meaning as "law."

> this rule = the law of gravity
> ∴ rule = law

Exercise 5–2

Directions: *Here are some more sentences. Look for the synonym of each underlined word in the sentences and write the synonym in the space. The first one is done for you.*

1. There are far more small business <u>firms</u> than large corporations. However, the large corporations make much more money than these small companies.

   firms = ____*companies*____

2. There are three <u>major</u> political ideologies in the world today: capitalism, socialism, and communism. Of course there are other types of ideologies as well, but these are the main types.

   major = _____

3. We keep our <u>ancient</u> Egyptian coins in a special case. We cannot take them out into the air to show them to you because these coins are very, very old.

   ancient = _____

4. American English and Canadian English are <u>nearly</u> the same. There are a few differences in pronunciation, but these two forms of English are almost the same.

   nearly = _____

5. David Johnson started his company in 1969. When the firm <u>began</u>, it was very small and employed only two workers.

   began = _____

6. You should repair that broken window. If you do not fix it soon, someone will be hurt.

   repair = _____

7. The Johnson Manufacturing Company makes water pumps for farms. Johnson Manufacturing produces 4000 water pumps every year.

   produces = _____

8. David Johnson wants his company to make high-quality products. Farmers will pay more for Johnson Water Pumps if they know that these are high-quality goods.

   products = _____

Antonyms in Context: Sometimes a writer gives information about the meaning of a new word by using an antonym in another sentence. In these sentences, we can find information about the word "began" because the writer uses an antonym in the second sentence.

   The Gold Rush began when gold was discovered in California. It ended when people learned that there was no more gold to find.

   began ≠ ended

   EXPLANATION:

   These sentences give us two kinds of information about the Gold Rush: It *began* when gold was discovered, and it *ended* when there was no more gold to find. We know that "gold was discovered" and "there was no more gold to find" have opposite meanings, so we can guess that "began" and "ended" have opposite meanings.

   began when gold was discovered ≠ ended when there was no more gold to find

   gold was discovered ≠ no more gold to find

   ∴ began ≠ ended

Exercise 5–3

Directions: *Here are some more sentences. Look for the antonym of each underlined word and write the antonym in the space. The first one is done for you.*

1. Gold traders sell gold when the price is high. Conversely, they buy gold when the price is low.
   sell ≠   *buy*
   _____

2. <u>Ancient</u> astronomers studied only the stars they could see with their eyes. With radio telescopes and satellites, however, modern astronomers can study stars which our eyes cannot see.

   ancient ≠ _____

3. It is very easy to <u>start</u> a job; it is much more difficult to finish one.

   start ≠ _____

4. Pollution is not considered a <u>major</u> problem in our country. On the contrary, we consider it a rather <u>minor</u> problem.

   major ≠ _____

5. High prices generally <u>hurt</u> consumers more than they hurt the producers. At the same time, high prices can often help the producers make more goods for the consumers to buy.

   hurt ≠ _____

6. If the farmers do not grow enough food this year, we will have a food <u>shortage</u>. On the other hand, we will have a food surplus if they grow too much food for the consumers to buy.

   shortage ≠ _____

Recognizing Prefixes with Opposite Meanings

In Unit 3 Word Study, we studied the following prefixes that add meaning to a word:

Prefix	Meaning	Example
re-	"again"	rewrite
pre-	"before"	prehistoric
post-	"after"	postwar
anti-	"against"	antisocial
mis-	"wrongly"	misspell
non-	"without"	nonstop

We also studied the following *negative* prefixes that have the meaning "not":

dis-	"not"	disagree
un-	"not"	unusual
in-	"not"	incomplete
im-	"not"	impossible

Sometimes writers use these negative prefixes to change words to their opposite meaning.

EXAMPLES:

happy   →   <u>un</u>happy (not happy)
similar   →   <u>dis</u>similar (not similar)
correct   →   <u>in</u>correct (not correct)
possible   →   <u>im</u>possible (not possible)

Sometimes two words can have opposite meanings because their **prefixes** have opposite meanings.

EXAMPLES:

<u>in</u>side   ≠   <u>out</u>side
<u>im</u>port   ≠   <u>ex</u>port
<u>in</u>crease ≠   <u>de</u>crease
<u>in</u>ternal ≠   <u>ex</u>ternal

Exercise 5–4

Directions: *Look at the diagrams to discover the meanings of these words with opposite meanings. Then complete the following sentences by writing the correct word in each space. The first one is done for you.*

FIGURE 5–1   Prefixes and opposite meanings

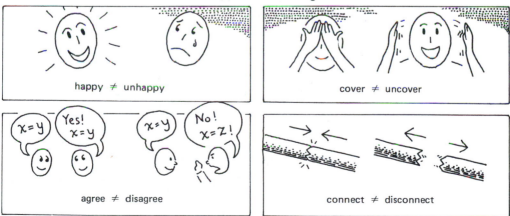

happy ≠ unhappy

cover ≠ uncover

agree ≠ disagree

connect ≠ disconnect

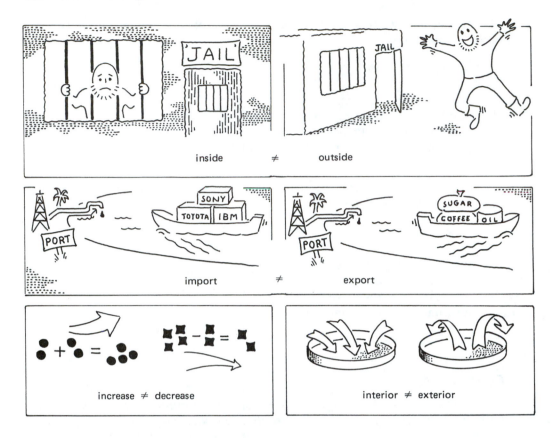

inside   ≠   outside

import   ≠   export

increase ≠ decrease

interior ≠ exterior

1. **(connect/disconnect)**   I must _____*disconnect*_____ the electricity
   before I repair this lamp. I will _____*connect*_____ the
   electricity again when I finish.

2. **(indoor/outdoor)**   The Recreation Center has two swimming pools, an
   indoor pool and an outdoor pool. We use the _____
   pool in the summer when the weather is warm, and we use the
   _____ pool in the winter when the weather is cold.

3. **(internal/external)**   The _____ Affairs Officer
   works with people inside the company, and the
   _____ Affairs Officer works with people outside the
   company.

4. **(import/export)** In our country, we _____ cars, televisions, and computers from other countries, and we

_____ oil, coffee, and sugar to other countries.

5. **(lock/unlock)** We always _____ our door at night,

but if you ring the bell we will _____ the door so that you can come in.

6. **(inflate/deflate)** You can _____ a football by

pumping air into the ball, but the ball will _____ if there is a hole in it.

7. **(inhale/exhale)** When you _____, you push air out

of your lungs; when you _____, you pull air into your lungs.

8. **(cover/uncover)** Be sure to _____ the lens of the

camera before you take the photograph, and _____ the lens with the lens cap after you take the photograph.

9. **(increase/decrease)** Use English every day and your vocabulary will

_____. However, your vocabulary will

_____ if you do not use English regularly.

10. **(prefix/suffix)** A _____ comes at the end of a

word, and a _____ comes at the beginning of a word.

Identifying the Part of Speech of a Word in Context to Select the Correct Dictionary Definition

When you look up a word in the dictionary, you will often find many definitions for the word. One way to find the correct definition is to find the part of speech of the word. Is it a noun, a verb, an adjective, or an adverb?

Noun or Verb? In Unit 1 Word Study we learned that some words have different noun and verb forms, but other words have the same noun and verb form. If a word has the same noun and verb form, we must look at the sentence to tell if the word is a noun or a verb.

EXAMPLE:

a. The *rent* for this apartment is $750 per month.

b. We can *rent* a car when we arrive at the airport.

In sentence a., "rent" is a noun, and in sentence b., "rent" is a verb. Two things tell us that "rent" is a noun in sentence a.: it is the subject of the sentence, and the word "the" comes before it. Three things tell us that "rent" is a verb in sentence b.: it comes between the subject and the object of the sentence, it tells us what the subject does, and the word "can" comes before it. (See Unit 1 Sentence Study for an explanation of "subject," "verb," and "object.")

In my dictionary, I find three definitions for "rent":

rent (rent) *n.* (L. *reditta*, paid) a stated payment at fixed intervals for the use of a house, land, etc.—*vt.* to get or give use of in return for rent—*vi.* to be let for rent—'rent•er *n.*

The definition of "rent" in sentence a. is the definition of "rent" as a noun (*n.*): "a stated payment at fixed intervals for use of a house, land, etc." (If you do not understand some of the words in the definition, you can look them up in your English dictionary or your bilingual dictionary.) To find the definition for "rent' in sentence b., we must first know the meanings of the abbreviations *vt.* and *vi.* (An abbreviation is a short form of a word or a group of words.) The list of "Abbreviations Used in this Dictionary" says that *vt.* means "transitive verb—a verb that can have an object"; and *vi.* means "intransitive verb—a verb that cannot have an object." In sentence b., "rent" has an object ("a car"), so the correct definition of "rent" in this sentence is the definition of "rent" as a transitive verb (*vt.*): "to get or give use of in return for rent."

Exercise 5-5

Directions: *Read the following sentences. Is the underlined word a noun or a verb? Look up the underlined word in your English dictionary and find the correct definition of the word for the sentence. Write the correct definition in the space. Then discuss your definitions with other students in your class.*

1. A <u>change</u> in the price of a product will affect the sale of that product.

    change: _____

2. Renters' unions <u>claim</u> that the government does not give enough help to renters.

    claim: _____

3. This year we have a lot of food, but the people in the Western Region do not have enough food. Therefore we will <u>share</u> our food with them.

   share: _____

4. An <u>increase</u> in food prices makes workers ask their employers for more money.

   increase: _____

5. The consumers <u>blame</u> the producers for the high prices, and the producers <u>blame</u> the unions.

   blame: _____

6. The new government price <u>controls</u> will help the consumers.

   controls: _____

7. Government leaders often <u>decrease</u> taxes before an election.

   decrease: _____

Noun or Adjective? Some words have the same noun and adjective form.
EXAMPLE:

  a. My friend Bruce is writing a *novel*.
  b. This book has some *novel* ideas for making money.

In my dictionary, I find two definitions for "novel":

  nov·el (näv′l) *adj*. (L. dim of *novus*, new) new and unusual—*n*. a relatively long fictional prose narrative

In sentence a., "novel" is a noun—it is the object of the sentence and the word "a" comes before it—so the correct definition for this sentence is "a relatively long fictional prose narrative." In sentence b., "novel" is an adjective—it gives information about the noun "ideas"—so the correct definition for sentence b. is "new and unusual." (Again, if you do not understand some of the words in the definitions, look them up in your English dictionary or your bilingual dictionary.)

Exercise 5-6

Directions: *Read the following sentences. Is the underlined word a noun or an adjective? Look up the underlined word in your English dictionary and find the correct definition of the word for the sentence. Write the correct definition in the space. Then discuss your definitions with other students in your class.*

1. He is the <u>equal</u> of Albert Einstein in intelligence.

   equal: _____

2. The Beatles sang, "In the end, the love you take is <u>equal</u> to the love you make."

   equal: _____

3. We saw many new products at the trade <u>fair</u> this year.

   fair: _____

4. My country exports many things, but our <u>major</u> export is oil.

   major: _____

5. The new tax law is not <u>fair</u> because it helps the rich people and hurts the poor people.

   fair: _____

6. I am a student at Northwestern University and my <u>major</u> is civil engineering.

   major: _____

7. Consumers do not like to pay <u>high</u> prices for goods.

   high: _____

8. Consumer prices reached a new <u>low</u> last month.

   low: _____

9. Our new ambassador is an <u>intellectual</u>. She has written several books about philosophy.

   intellectual: _____

10. In an <u>ideal</u> society, people have the freedom to do what they want and the discipline to use their freedom correctly.

    ideal: _____

Sentence Study

Identifying Modifying Clauses and Phrases

Writers often use signal words like "and," "but," "however," "although," "so," and "therefore" to put more information into their sentences (see Unit 1 and Unit 3 Sentence Study). Writers also use *modifying clauses and phrases** to put more information into their sentences.

Modifying Clauses and Phrases of Time: Here are some sentences with modifying clauses and phrases. In these sentences the modifying clauses and phrases give us information about the *time* in the sentences.

1. People buy more goods *when prices are low.*

   Information: people buy more goods

   Time: *when* prices are low

2. *When prices are high,* they buy less.

   Information: they buy less

   Time: *when* prices are high

3. *As the prices of goods go up,* producers make more goods.

   Information: producers make more goods

   Time: *as* the prices of goods go up

4. *In 1872,* Samuel Butler wrote a novel.

   Information: Samuel Butler wrote a novel

   Time: *in* 1872

5. Many utopian communities began *during the 1800s.*

   Information: Many utopian communities began

   Time: *during* the 1800s

   (*Note:* "the 1800s" means the years from 1800 to 1899.)

6. *After the rent increase,* many renters moved out of their apartments.

   Information: many renters moved out of their apartments

   Time: *after* the rent increase

7. Few cities had rent control *before World War II.*

   Information: few cities had rent control

   Time: *before* World War II

In the preceding sentences, the modifying clauses and phrases begin with signal words. These signal words—*when, as, in, during, after,* and *before*—tell

---

*A *clause* is a group of words with a subject and a verb. Every sentence has one or more clauses. For example, an SVO sentence has only one clause, and an SVO + SVO sentence has two clauses. (See Unit 1 Sentence Study for an explanation of "SVO sentence" and "SVO + SVO sentence.") A *phrase* is also a group of words, but a phrase does not have a subject and a verb.

us that the modifying clause or phrase gives information about the *time* in the sentence.

Exercise 5-7

Directions: *Here are some more sentences with modifying clauses and phrases of time. Read the sentences and <u>underline</u> the modifying clauses and phrases of time. The first sentence is done for you.*

People buy less <u>when prices are high</u>. <u>As prices go down</u>, they buy more.

Rent control in the United States began in 1943. Few American cities had rent control before World War II. During World War II, the U.S. government imposed rent control on all American cities. After World War II, only one city—New York—continued rent control. At the beginning of the 1980s, nearly one fifth of the people in the U.S. lived in cities with rent control.

Modifying Clauses and Phrases of Cause, Result, and Purpose: Here are some more sentences with modifying clauses and phrases. These modifying clauses and phrases give us different kinds of information about the sentences. The signal word at the beginning of the clause or phrase tells us what kind of information the clause or phrase gives.

1. Apartments are expensive *because there are not enough apartments for people to rent.*

   Information: apartments are expensive

   Cause: *because* there are not enough apartments for people to rent

2. We will not buy your product *because of the high price.*

   Information: we will not buy your product

   Cause: *because of* the high price

3. There are not enough apartments for people to rent; *as a result, apartments are expensive.*

   Information: there are not enough apartments for people to rent

   Result: *as a result* apartments are expensive

4. The price of your product is too high, *so we will not buy it.*

   Information: the price of your product is too high

   Result: *so* we will not buy it

5. Workers are moving to the city *in order to find work.*

   Information: workers are moving to the city

   Purpose: *in order to* find work

6. Workers are moving to the city *so that they can find work.*

   Information workers are moving to the city

   Purpose: *so that* they can find work

In these sentences, the modifying clauses and phrases tell us about the *causes, results,* and *purposes* of the information in the sentences. The signal words *because* and *because of* tell us that the clause or phrase gives the *cause* of the information in the sentence. The signal words *as a result* and *so* tell us that the clause or phrase gives the *result* of the information in the sentence. The signal words *so that* and *in order to* tell us that the clause or phrase gives the *purpose* of the information in the sentence.

Exercise 5-8

Directions: *Read these sentences and underline the modifying clauses and phrases that tell us about the* causes, results, *or* purposes *of the information in the sentences. The first one is done for you.*

When the prices of goods are high, producers can make more money, <u>so they make more goods</u>. However, consumers will not buy more goods because of the high prices. Consumers will only buy more when the price is low; as a result, the prices must go down. Producers make more goods so that the consumers will buy more goods. At the same time, producers must keep the prices low in order to sell more goods.

Modifying Clauses and Phrases that Give Information about a Noun: Here are some more sentences with modifying clauses and phrases. These clauses and phrases give information about a noun in the sentence.

1. A renter is a person *who rents a house or an apartment.*

   Noun: a *person*

   Information about the noun: *who* rents a house or an apartment

2. *Sir Thomas More* wrote a novel about a perfect country, *which he named Utopia.*

   Noun: a perfect *country*

   Information about the noun: *which* he named Utopia

3. Utopia is a place *where everything is perfect.*

   Noun: a *place*

   Information about the noun: *where* everything is perfect

4. Albert Einstein, *the famous physicist,* once failed mathematics in high school.

Noun: Albert Einstein

Information about the noun: the famous physicist

5. A clause is a group of words *with a subject and a verb*.

Noun: a *group* of words

Information about the noun: *with* a subject and a verb
(*Note:* "*with* a subject and a verb" tells us what is included in a "group of words.")

6. A phrase is a group of words *without a subject and a verb*.

Noun: a *group* of words

Information about the noun: *without* a subject and a verb
(*Note:* "*without* a subject and a verb" tells us what is *not* included in "a group of words.")

Exercise 5-9

Directions: *Read these sentences and <u>underline</u> the modifying clauses and phrases that give information about a noun. The first one is done for you.*

Modern Times was the name of a nineteenth century anarchist community. "Anarchy" is a Greek word <u>that means "without a leader."</u> An anarchist is a person who thinks that all governments are bad. Pierre Joseph Proudhon, the French philosopher, was the first anarchist. He believed that a government with a leader is bad for the people. An anarchist community is a place where there are no leaders, so Modern Times was a community without a leader.

Modifying Clauses and Phrases of Place, Example, Source, and Condition: Here are some more sentences with modifying clauses and phrases. The signal word at the beginning of the clause or phrase tells us what kind of information the clause or phrase gives.

1. *In most American cities,* the rent for an apartment is more than $250 per month.

Information: the rent for an apartment is more than $250 per month

Place of the information: *in* most American cities

2. Apartments are more expensive in large cities; *for example, apartments in New York City rent for more than $700.*

Information: apartments are more expensive in large cities

Example of the information: *for example,* apartments in New York City rent for more than $700.

3. Apartments are more expensive in large cities *such as New York.*

   Information: apartments are more expensive in large cities

   Example of the information: *such as* New York

4. *According to the law of gravity,* everything falls toward the center of the earth.

   Information: everything falls toward the center of the earth

   Source of the information: *according to* the law of gravity

5. *If you live in New York City,* you must pay at least $700 a month to rent an apartment.

   Information: you must pay at least $700 a month to rent an apartment

   What is necessary to make the information true: *if* you live in New York City

   ("You must pay at least $700 a month to rent an apartment" is not true in all cities, but it is true "if you live in New York City.")

Exercise 5-10

Directions: *Read these sentences and* <u>underline</u> *the modifying clauses and phrases. The first one is done for you.*

According to a 1980 survey, the rent for a one-bedroom apartment is more than $250 in most American cities. In some of the smaller cities such as Louisville, Kentucky or Jacksonville, Florida, the rent is less, but in larger cities the rent is more. For example, you must pay $400 or more to rent a one-bedroom Los Angeles apartment, and the same apartment rents for $625 and up in Chicago. If you are a renter, the most expensive city in the U.S. is New York, where you must pay at least $700 a month for a one-bedroom apartment.

Exercise 5-11

Directions: *Read the following sentences. Each sentence has one modifying clause or phrase.* <u>Underline</u> *the modifying clause or phrase. What kind of information about the sentence does the modifying clause or phrase give? Write the kind of information in the space. If you need help, look at Table 5-1. The first sentence is done for you.*

1. A builder is a person <u>who builds houses or buildings.</u>

   Kind of information: _____*information about a noun*_____

2. If producers make too many goods, the consumers cannot buy all of the goods.

   Kind of information: _____

TABLE 5–1 Signal Words for Modifying Clauses and Phrases

Time	Cause	Purpose	Information about a Noun
when	because	so that	who
as	because of	in order to	which
in			where
during	**Result**	**Example**	with
after	as a result	for example	without
before	so	such as	
	Place	**Source**	
	in	according to	

What is Necessary to Make the Information True

if

3. Workers try to find better jobs in the cities.

   Kind of information: _____

4. Some families move into apartments when the rent for their houses increases.

   Kind of information: _____

5. Utopia has no banks because the people of Utopia do not need money.

   Kind of information: _____

6. Rent-control laws help people who cannot pay high rents.

   Kind of information: _____

7. During World War II, the U.S. government imposed rent controls.

   Kind of information: _____

8. The government imposed rent controls in order to help the families of workers and soldiers.

   Kind of information: _____

9. After the war, only one city—New York—continued the rent controls.

   Kind of information: _____

10. Today there are many cities with rent-control laws.

   Kind of information: _____

Synonymous Sentences

Sometimes different modifying clauses and phrases have the same meaning. For example, these three sentences have the same meaning:

A city is a place *where at least 100,000 people live.*

A city is a place *which has at least 100,000 people.*

A city is a place *with at least 100,000 people.*

"Where at least 100,000 people live," "which has at least 100,000 people," and "with at least 100,000 people" all give the *same* information about the sentence.

Sometimes a writer changes the place of a modifying clause or phrase in a sentence. Usually this does not change the meaning. For example, these three sentences have the same meaning:

In most American cities, the rent for a one-bedroom apartment is more than $250 per month.

The rent for a one-bedroom apartment *in most American cities* is more than $250 per month.

The rent for a one-bedroom apartment is more than $250 per month *in most American cities.*

If a writer changes the place of a *signal word* in the sentence, or if a writer uses a different signal word, this sometimes changes the meaning.

EXAMPLES:

These three sentences have the *same* meaning:

1. We will not buy your product *because the price is too high.*

2. *Because the price is too high,* we will not buy your product.

3. The price is too high, *so we will not buy your product.*

These three sentences have *different* meanings:

1. We will not buy your product *because the price is too high.*

2. *Because we will not buy your product,* the price is too high.

3. We will not buy your product *if the price is too high.*

Exercise 5–12

Directions: *Look at the following groups of sentences. One sentence has the same meaning as the first sentence in the group. Find the sentence with the same meaning and put a check (✓) beside it. The first one is done for you.*

1. Producers produce more goods so that they can make more money.

    ___✓___ a. In order to make more money, producers produce more goods.

    _____ b. Producers produce more goods after they make more money.

    _____ c. With more money, producers produce more goods.

2. If the prices of goods are very high, people will not buy the goods.

    _____ a. People will not buy the goods, so the prices of the goods are very high.

    _____ b. People will not buy the goods if the prices of the goods are very high.

    _____ c. The prices of the goods are very high because people will not buy the goods.

3. People buy more goods as the prices of goods go down.

    _____ a. When the prices of goods go down, people buy more goods.

    _____ b. Because people buy more goods, the prices of goods go down.

    _____ c. People buy more goods where the prices of goods go down.

4. Utopia is a place where the people all work together and share.

    _____ a. If Utopia is a place, the people will work together and share.

    _____ b. Utopia is a place; for example, the people all work together and share.

    _____ c. In Utopia all of the people work together and share.

5. Utopia is a place where there is no war, no poverty, no hunger, and no crime.

    _____ a. Utopia is not without war, proverty, hunger, or crime.

    _____ b. Utopia is a place which has war, poverty, hunger, and crime.

    _____ c. Utopia is a place without war, poverty, hunger, or crime.

6. Hotel prices increase during the summer when the tourists come.

    _____ a. If hotel prices increase during the summer, the tourists come.

    _____ b. The tourists come in the summer, so hotels raise their prices then.

_____ c. Because hotel prices increase during the summer, the tourists come.

7. The city will impose rent-control laws so that it can help low-income families.

    _____ a. The city will impose rent-control laws in order to help low-income families.

    _____ b. The city can help low-income families; as a result, it will impose rent controls.

    _____ c. The city will impose rent-control laws when it can help low-income families.

8. It is very expensive to rent a house; as a result, many young families live in apartments.

    _____ a. It is very expensive to rent a house as many young families live in apartments.

    _____ b. Because it is very expensive to rent a house, many young families live in apartments.

    _____ c. It is very expensive to rent a house if many young families live in apartments.

Paragraph Study

Identifying Topic Sentences

Every paragraph has a topic and a main idea (see Unit 3 Paragraph Study). Many paragraphs have topic sentences. The *topic sentence* of a paragraph (sometimes called the "main idea sentence") is one which identifies both the topic and the main idea of a paragraph.

EXAMPLE:

Directions: *Here is a paragraph with a topic sentence. Read the paragraph and look for the topic sentence. Then answer the question.*

When you rent an apartment, it is important to have an apartment lease. A lease is an agreement between the owner of the apartment and you, the renter. It tells you the amount of rent for the apartment, and it gives you information about when and where you must pay the rent. It also tells you how long you can live in the apartment. A lease helps the owner of the apartment, but it also helps the renter. If you sign a lease, the owner cannot increase the rent or tell you to leave the apartment without a good reason.

What is the topic sentence of this paragraph?

a. When you rent an apartment, it is important to have an apartment lease.

b. A lease is an agreement between the owner of the apartment and you, the renter.

c. If you sign a lease before you move into an apartment, the owner cannot increase the rent or tell you to leave the apartment without a good reason.

(The correct answer is a.)

EXPLANATION:

Answer a. is correct because this sentence tells us what the topic of the paragraph is ("an apartment lease"), and it tells us what the main idea of the paragraph is. (All of the sentences tell us why it is important to have an apartment lease.)

Answer b. is not correct because this sentence does not tell us what *all* of the sentences in the paragraph say about the topic. All of the sentences tell us why it is important to have an apartment lease, but this sentence only tells us what a lease is.

Answer c. is not correct because this sentence gives us only *two* reasons why it is important to have an apartment lease. The paragraph gives us *seven* reasons why it is important to have an apartment lease:

1. It is an agreement between the owner and the renter.
2. It tells you how much the rent is.
3. It tells you when and where you must pay the rent.
4. It tells you how long you can live in the apartment.
5. It helps the owner, but it also helps the renter.
6. The owner cannot increase the rent without a good reason.
7. The owner cannot tell you to leave without a good reason.

When a paragraph has a topic sentence, it is usually the first sentence in the paragraph. For this reason, it is a good idea to read the first sentence of every paragraph very carefully.

However, the topic sentence is sometimes at the end of a paragraph, and sometimes it is in the middle of the paragraph. Look at these paragraphs. The topic sentence of each paragraph is <u>underlined</u>.

1. <u>Changes in the prices of goods can cause changes in production and consumption.</u> Production increases when the prices are high. As the prices of goods go up, producers make more goods because they can make more money when they sell the goods. On the other hand, consumption increases when the

prices are low. As the prices of goods go down, consumers buy more goods because of the low prices.

2. Producers make more goods when prices are high, and consumers buy more goods when prices are low. As prices go up, producers make more goods because they can make more money for their goods. As prices go down, consumers buy more goods because of the low prices. This shows us how changes in the prices of goods can cause changes in production and consumption.

3. When prices are high, producers can get more money for their goods. When prices are low, consumers can get more goods for their money. These changes in the prices of goods can cause changes in production and consumption. As the prices of goods go up, producers will make more goods in order to make more money. As the prices go down, consumers will buy more goods because of the low prices.

Exercise 5-13

Directions: *Here are some more paragraphs with topic sentences. Underline the topic sentence in each paragraph. The first one is done for you. When you finish, discuss your answers with other students in your class.*

1. In 1814, George Rapp started a utopian community in Harmony, Indiana. In 1824, Rapp sold the community to Robert Owen, who started a new utopian community there. He named the new community "New Harmony." New Harmony lasted only two years. In 1825, Francis Wright started the community of Nashoba near Memphis, Tennessee. The Nashoba community ended in 1830. Brook farm, a utopian farming community, lasted from 1841 to 1847. Modern Times, an anarchist community near New York City, was started by Josiah Warren in 1851. It ended in 1857. We can see that these utopian communities that started in the 1800s lasted only a short time.

2. The price of a box of Wonder Soap is $1.95, and the price of a box of Super Soap is $2.15. Which box of soap are you going to buy? Many people will buy the box of Wonder Soap because of the low price. However, it is important to know the *real* price of goods before you buy. There are sixteen ounces (450 grams) of soap in the box of Wonder Soap, but there are twenty-one ounces (almost 600 grams) of soap in the box of Super Soap. The *real* price of the Wonder Soap is $0.12 per ounce and the *real* price of the Super Soap is $0.10 per ounce, so the price of the Super Soap is really lower than the price of the Wonder Soap.

3. Many apartment-renting services are using computers to help people find apartments. They find out important information about the apartments

such as the number of bedrooms, the location, and the amount of rent. They put this information into the computer. When a person comes to the apartment-renting service, questions are asked about the kind of apartment the person wants. This information is put into the computer, and the computer "finds" the best apartment for the person.

4. It is easy to find out the prices of goods, but what are the costs of the goods? Many consumers think that "price" and "cost" are the same, but they are mistaken. The price is the amount of money the consumer must pay in order to buy the goods, but the cost is the amount of money the producer must pay in order to make the goods. If a producer is making shoes, for example, the producer must buy leather, thread, glue, and sewing machines in order to make the shoes. The producer must also pay the workers who make the shoes. The money for leather, thread, glue, sewing machines, and workers is the *cost* of making the shoes. Then the producer decides the *price* of the shoe. The price is always higher than the cost because some money must go to the producer for making the shoes.

5. When you decide to rent an apartment, you should first look at the apartment very carefully. Look at the walls, the ceiling, and the doors. Look at the furniture (beds, chairs, tables, etc.) and look at the appliances (refrigerator, stove, washing machine, etc.) If you find anything broken, ask the owner to fix it before you move in. Next, you should read the lease very carefully. If you do not understand the lease, ask someone to explain it to you. Finally, sign the lease and keep your copy of it in a safe place. If you follow these steps, you will be much happier with your new apartment.

Dividing Information According to Time, Place, and Causal Relationship

Writers organize information in a paragraph in different ways. Sometimes they use *time* organization, sometimes they use *place* organization, and sometimes they use *cause and result* organization.

Read the following paragraphs and look at the notes. The notes will show how the writer organized the paragraphs.

Time Organization

Rent control began fairly recently in the United States. Few American cities had rent control before World War II. During World War II, the U.S. government imposed rent control on all the cities in the U.S. After World War II, only one city—New York—continued rent control. At the beginning of the 1980s nearly one fifth of the people in the U.S. lived in cities with rent control.

NOTES: (time)	(information about rent control)
Before World War II:	Few cities had rent control.
During World War II:	All cities had rent control.
After World War II:	Only New York continued rent control.
Beginning of 1980s:	Nearly one fifth of the people in the U.S. had rent control.

Place Organization

The cost of renting an apartment varies from one American city to another. In most cities, the rent for a one-bedroom apartment is more than $250 per month. In some smaller cities such as Louisville, Kentucky or Jacksonville, Florida, the rent is less, but in larger cities the rent is more. For example, if you live in Los Angeles, you must pay $400 or more to rent a one-bedroom apartment, and the same apartment rents for $625 and up in Chicago. The most expensive rents in the U.S. are in New York, where you must pay at least $700 a month to rent a one-bedroom apartment in most parts of the city.

NOTES: (place)	(rent for one-bedroom apartment)
Most American cities:	> $250
Smaller cities:	< $250
Louisville	
Jacksonville	
Larger cities:	> $250
Los Angeles:	≥ $400
Chicago:	≥ $625
New York:	≥ $700

Cause and Result Organization

The prices of shoes are related to the number of shoes the producers make. For example, the price of shoes was high last month, so the shoe producers made more shoes. However, the consumers did not buy more shoes because of the high price. As a result, the shoe producers reduced the price of the shoes so that the consumers could buy more shoes. At the same time, the shoe producers reduced their production of shoes because the prices went down.

NOTES: (cause)		(result)
price of shoes↑	→	shoe production ↑
high price	→	consumers did not buy more
consumers did not buy more	→	price of shoes↓
price of shoes↓	→	consumers could buy more
price of shoes↓	→	shoe production↓

Exercise 5-14

Directions: *Here are some more paragraphs with notes, but the notes are not complete. Read the paragraphs and complete the notes. The first one is done for you.*

1. A number of utopian communities sprang up in the United States during the last century. In 1814, George Rapp started a utopian community in Harmony, Indiana. In 1824, Rapp sold the community to Robert Owen, who started a new utopian community there. He named the new community "New Harmony." New Harmony lasted only two years. In 1825, Francis Wright started the community of Nashoba near Memphis, Tennessee. The Nashoba community ended in 1830. Brook Farm, a utopian farming community, lasted from 1841 to 1847. Modern Times, an anarchist community near New York City, was started by Josiah Warren in 1851. It ended in 1857.

NOTES:	(time)	(utopian community)
	1814–1824	*Harmony*
	1824–1826	*New Harmony*
	1825–1830	*Nashoba*
	1841–1847	*Brook Farm*
	1851–1857	*Modern Times*

2. The space race between the U.S. and the Soviet Union has had its "ups and downs." From 1957 to 1969, the Soviet Union was "first in space." The Soviet Union launched Sputnik 1, the first space satellite, on October 4, 1957, and Yuri Gagarin, the Russian cosmonaut, became the first person to orbit the earth on April 12, 1961. The United States became "first in space" in 1969, when Apollo 11 landed on the moon with two American astronauts on July 20. The United States launched the first space station, Skylab, in 1973. The Soviet Union and the United States worked together in space on July 17, 1975, when two Russian cosmonauts and two American astronauts had the first international meeting in space. After the meeting, the Soviet Union worked mostly on space stations such as Salyut 6 and Salyut 7, and the United States worked mostly on space shuttles such as Columbia and Challenger.

NOTES:

(time)	(information)
1957–1969:	*Soviet Union "first in space"*

Oct. 4, 1957: _____

April 12, 1961: _____

1969:   **_United States "first in space"_** _____

July 20, 1969: _____

1973: _____

July 17, 1975: _____

_____

After the meeting: Soviet Union _____

United States _____

3. There are more old people in the world today because of an increase in medical services in the world. Today, more people can get medical services from doctors and nurses in hospitals and clinics. As a result, fewer people get fatal diseases such as yellow fever, malaria, cholera, and typhoid. This decrease in fatal diseases causes a decrease in the number of people who die from these diseases. Because of this decrease in the number of deaths, people can live longer today. As a result, there has been an increase in the number of old people living in the world today.

NOTES: **(causes)**   **(results)**

↑ medical services   →   ↑ old people

↑ medical services   →   _____

↓ fatal diseases   →   _____

↓ deaths   →   _____

people live longer   →   _____

4. We can divide the world into two parts: the "north" (Europe, North America, Japan, etc.) and the "south" (Asia, Africa, Latin America, etc.). Most of the people in the world live in the south, but the people in the north have most of the money and services. According to the Overseas Development Council, there are 3.4 billion people in the south and only 1.1 billion people in the north. People in the north have an average income of $6,468 per year, but the income of people in the south is $597 per year. The countries of the north pay $286 per person for education every year, and 99 percent of the people in the north can read and write. The countries of the south pay $18 per person for education every year, and only 52 percent of the people can read and write. The countries of the north pay $199 per person for medical services, and most

of the people in the north live to be 72 years old. The countries of the south pay $6.50 per person for medical services, and most of the people live to be only 56 years old. The leaders of the north and south must work together to share the money and services of the world more equally.

NOTES: Two parts of the world:

	North	South
	most money and services	*most people*
people:		
income:	_____	_____
education:	_____	_____
people who can read and write:	_____	_____
medical services:	_____	_____
people live to be:	_____	_____

Conclusion: _____

_____

Reading Speed

Rapid Recognition of Identical Words and Phrases

Exercise 5–15

Directions: *Look at the first word. Then look at the other words on the same line. Find the first word and circle it. You may find the first word more than one time.*

EXAMPLE:

cost   cast   coast (cost) lost   cattle (cost) cast

1. (suggested time: 20 seconds)

must most mist mast must much most mush much

price prize price praise place price prose prize

firm fern farm form from firm fire film firm

<u>major</u> mayor major magic minor wager major mayor

<u>personal</u> personal personality personnel person personally

<u>real</u> read real real reel rail reed reel read

<u>change</u> change charge chance charge glance change charge

2. (suggested time: 20 seconds)

<u>share</u> shave share shove share stare slave shave share

<u>lasted</u> listed fasted lasting lasted listed lasted fasten

<u>founded</u> found funded founded floundered founded funded

<u>when</u> when then where when whom which when then wren

<u>who</u> who why how whom how who why who two wow

<u>clause</u> cause clause close cause choose class claws

<u>apartment</u> agreement apartment department apartment argument

<u>intersect</u> inspect interject interest intersect intersect

<u>signal</u> single signed signal single signal several signed

Exercise 5–16

Directions: *Look at the key phrase. Then look at the other phrases in the "paragraph." Find the key phrase and circle it. You may find the key phrase more than one time in the "paragraph."*

EXAMPLE:

Key phrase: **a perfect place**

(a perfect place) a personal palace a person's face (a perfect place) the perfect palace (a perfect place) (a perfect place) a personal place the person's pace a perfect sphere (a perfect place) a preferred place (a perfect place) protect a place perfect the place a perfected plan (a perfect place)

How many times did you find the key phrase?   _7_

1. Key phrase: **a good idea** (suggested time: 30 seconds)

a bad idea a good idea a good deal a food idea a good idea

a bad deal a good idea a wooden idol a wood idea an ideal food

a good idea a long ordeal a pool idea a fool idea an idle foot
a good index a food idea a good idea a good idea an idle pool
a good deal a good ideal a good slide good eyes an ideal good
a good ideal a good idea

How many times did you find the key phrase? _____

2. Key phrase: **low-income families** (suggested time: 30 seconds)

low-income families high income families low-income fathers
one-income families low-income families low-increase families
two-income families low-income fathers low-income families less-
inclined families slow-income families low-incoming planes one-
income families low-income families two-income families slow-
growing families low-increase families

How many times did you find the key phrase? _____

3. Key phrase: **one-bedroom apartment** (suggested time: 30 seconds)

one-room apartment one-bedroom apartment one-bedroom department
one-room compartment one-room apartment one-bedroom apartment
two-bedroom apartment one-bedroom compartment one-bedroom apartment low-income apartment one-income apartment one-room apartment
one-bedroom apartment two-bedroom apartment one-bedroom department one-bedroom apartment

How many times did you find the key phrase? _____

4. Key phrase: **in order to** (suggested time: 30 seconds)

in order of on order to an order to in order to in order of an
over to an order of in order of on order to in order to in order
to on order to in order of in order to

How many times did you find the key phrase? _____

5. Key phrase: **on the other hand** (suggested time: 30 seconds)

on the one hand on the other hand in the other hand in another

land   in the other land   on the one hand   on the other hand   on the
left hand   on the order of   on the other hand   in the other land   in
the other hand   on the other hand   on the other hand   on the other
land   in the other hand   on the one hand   on the other hand   on the
other hand   on the order of   in the other hand

How many times did you find the key phrase? _____

6. Key phrase: **personal possessions** (suggested time: 30 seconds)

personal possessions   personnel positions   personal opposition
personal possessions   personal possessions   personal positions
opposite positions   private possessions   personnel positions
professional positions   personal positions   personal possessions

How many times did you find the key phrase? _____

Rapid Recognition of Synonyms

Exercise 5–17

Directions: *Look at the following pairs of words. Do they have* similar *meanings or* different *meanings? If the two words have similar meanings, circle the letter S. if they have different meanings, circle the letter D. Try to do this exercise as quickly as you can.*

EXAMPLES:

	start	begin	Ⓢ	D
	real	equal	S	Ⓓ
1.	firm	company	S	D
2.	goods	prices	S	D
3.	equal	nearly	S	D
4.	nearly	almost	S	D
5.	producer	consumer	S	D
6.	repair	fix	S	D
7.	intersect	interest	S	D
8.	increase	raise	S	D
9.	most	all	S	D
10.	major	real	S	D
11.	products	goods	S	D

12. ancient	old	S	D
13. novel	income	S	D
14. main	major	S	D
15. rent	repair	S	D
16. law	rule	S	D
17. cause	result	S	D
18. produce	make	S	D
19. increase	less	S	D

Now trade books with another student and check his or her answers.

Exercise 5–18

Directions: *Look at the first word. Then look at the other words on the line. Find the word with a similar meaning to the first word and circle it. Try to do this exercise as quickly as you can.*

EXAMPLE:

start   end   increase   (begin)   control   make

nearly   really   ancient   repair   produce   almost   most

increase   interest   raise   intersect   repair   major   real

goods   produces   prices   causes   makes   products   increase

major   main   minor   rent   rule   result   almost   most

company   income   product   consumer   firm   fix   intersect

share   repair   part   increase   main   goods   result

rule   cause   result   law   rent   produce   low   real

fix   repair   produce   major   intersect   result   raise

ancient   consumer   share   part   novel   result   real   old

make   increase   repair   produce   income   ancient   less

Now trade books with another student and check his or her answers.

Recognizing Synonyms in Context

In Unit 5 Word Study we discovered that writers sometimes give the meaning of a new word by using a synonym in another sentence. Writers also use synonyms when they do not want to use the same word more than one time in a sentence or paragraph.

EXAMPLE:

In this paragraph, the writer does not use synonyms. The writer uses the same word again and again.

Today, Duer Tool and Die Inc. is a *big* corporation. It is *big* because there is a *big* demand for its products. Like all *big* corporations, Duer Tool and Die faces *big* labor problems.

In the following paragraph, the writer uses synonyms. The writer does not use the same word more than one time.

Today, Duer Tool and Die Inc. is a *huge* corporation. It is *big* because there is a *large* demand for its products. Like all *giant* corporations, Duer Tool and Die faces *enormous* labor problems.

Exercise 5-19

Directions: *Look at the key word. Then read the sentences and look for words with similar meanings to the key word. Circle each word that has a similar meaning to the key word.*

EXAMPLE:

Key word: **produce**

Many companies *produce* computer games. For example, Atari and Intellivision both (make) their own computer games. Companies such as Apple and Radio Shack also (manufacture) games for their home computers.

1. Key word: **company**

The *company* she works for is Ace Chemicals. She joined the firm in 1965 when it was very small. Now Ace Chemicals is the largest business in the area.

2. Key word: **laws**

Anarchists are against the *laws* that governments imposed on people. They feel that these regulations take freedom away from the people. In fact, anarchists believe that rules hurt people more than they help people.

3. Key word: **major**

Cars are the *major* source of air pollution in some cities. In industrial cities, factories are the principal source of pollution. The main source of air pollution in my town, however, is smoke from cooking fires.

4. Key word: **started**

Jean Henri Dumant, a Swiss banker, *started* the International Red Cross in 1862. The Red Cross officially began at the Geneva Convention in 1864. Clara Barton, an American nurse, founded the American Red Cross in 1881.

5. Key word: **decrease**

Sometimes producers *decrease* their prices in order to sell their goods. When producers lower their prices, people will buy more goods. Producers do not like to reduce their prices, but sometimes it is necessary.

UNIT 6 Reading Passages

Supply and Demand

Photo by Cheri Wilder

Introduction

Sometimes prices are high, and sometimes they are low. Why do prices go up and down? There are no easy answers to this question. Prices change for many reasons. Governments, people in business, consumers, workers, bankers—all of these can cause changes in prices. Changes in technology, changes in philosophy, and even changes in the weather can make prices go up or down.

When economists talk about prices, they talk about supply and demand. The "Law of Supply and Demand" is a basic law of economics. It is a very simple law, but it can answer many questions about prices. In some countries business controls prices and in other countries government controls prices, but economists in all countries study supply and demand. In this chapter we will look at the Law of Supply and Demand in order to see how it explains changes in prices.

Vocabulary Preparation

Graphs: Figure 6–1, Figure 6–2, and Figure 6–3 in this chapter are called *graphs*. They give us information about changes in prices of shoes and in numbers of shoes made. Look at the graphs and answer these questions.

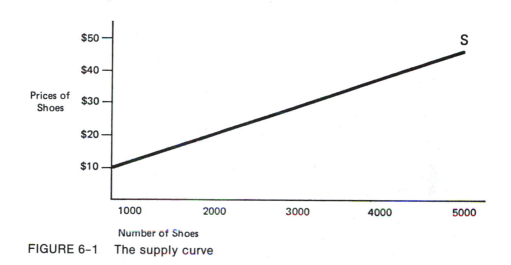

FIGURE 6–1   The supply curve

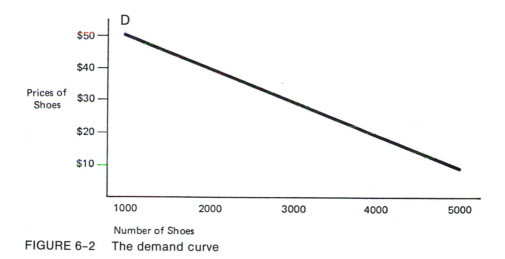

FIGURE 6–2   The demand curve

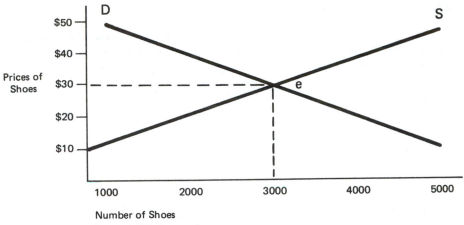

FIGURE 6-3   The equilibrium price

1. Line S in Figure 6-1 is the supply *curve,* and line D in Figure 6-2 is the demand *curve.*

   A curve is _____.
   a. a graph
   b. a line on a graph
   c. the number of shoes
   d. the prices of shoes

2. In Figure 6-3, line S and line D *intersect* at point e.

   Intersect means _____.
   a. begin
   b. end
   c. cross
   d. point

3. In Figure 6-1, curve S goes up. This means that the prices of shoes _____ as the number of shoes increases.

   a. increase
   b. decrease
   c. remain the same

4. In Figure 6-2, curve D goes down. This means that the prices of shoes _____ as the number of shoes increases.

a. increase

b. decrease

c. remain the same

Vocabulary in Context

Directions: *Read the sentences and guess the meaning of the underlined word or phrase. Then answer the question. Please do* not *use your dictionary.*

1. My uncle is a <u>shopkeeper</u>. He owns a small shoe store that specializes in ladies' shoes and sandals. At first he did all the work himself, but now he has two assistants to help him.

   A <u>shopkeeper</u> is a person who _____.

   a. works in a store

   b. owns a store

   c. sells shoes

   d. makes shoes and sandals

2. An increase in the prices of goods causes an increase in production. <u>At the same time</u>, it causes a decrease in consumption.

   <u>At the same time</u> tells us that the second sentence gives us more informa-

   tion about the results of _____.

   a. an increase in prices

   b. an increase in production

   c. a decrease in consumption

   d. a decrease in prices

3. An increase in the prices of goods causes an increase in production and a decrease in consumption. <u>Conversely</u>, a decrease in the prices of goods causes a decrease in production and an increase in consumption.

   <u>Conversely</u> tells us that the information in the second sentence is

   _____ the information in the first sentence.

   a. the same as

   b. similar to

   c. the result of

   d. opposite to

4. An increase in the price of shoes causes an increase in the production of shoes. This means that producers make <u>more</u> shoes when the price is high, and they make fewer shoes when the price is low.

Which word is the *antonym* (opposite in meaning) of <u>more</u>?

a. increase

b. high

c. fewer

d. low

5.

Ownership of Electronic Equipment
By Students of Podunk University

<u>Equipment</u>	<u>Percentage of Students</u>
Radio	100%
Calculator	98%
Television	85%
Home Computer	5%
Video Tape Recorder	0%

According to a recent survey, <u>all of</u> the students at Podunk University own radios. Almost all of the students own calculators, but not all of them own televisions. Only a few own home computers, and none of the students owns a video tape recorder.

Which phrase is the antonym (opposite in meaning) of <u>all of</u>?

a. almost all of

b. not all of

c. only a few

d. none of

Text

Supply and Demand

When prices are low people will buy more, and when prices are high they will buy less. Every shopkeeper knows this. But at the same time, producers want higher prices for their goods when they make more goods. How can we find the best price for the goods? The Law of Supply and Demand is the economist's answer to this question.

According to this law, changes in the prices of goods cause changes in supply and demand. An increase in the price of the goods causes an increase in *supply*—the number of goods the producers make. Producers will make more goods when they can get higher prices for the goods. In Figure 6–1, the producer makes more shoes as the price of shoes goes up. At the same time, an increase in the price of the goods causes a *decrease* in *demand*—the number of goods the consumers buy. This is because people buy less when the price is high. In Figure 6-2, people buy fewer shoes as the price of shoes goes up. Conversely, a decrease in the price causes an increase in demand (people buy more shoes) and a decrease in supply (producers make fewer shoes).

Business firms look at both supply and demand when they make decisions about prices and production. They look for the *equilibrium point* where supply equals demand. In Figure 6-3, the equilibrium point is point *e*, where the supply curve (S) and the demand curve (D) intersect. At this point, the number of shoes produced is 3000 and the price of the shoes is $30. $30 is the *equilibrium price:* at this price the consumers will buy all of the 3000 shoes which the producers make. If the producers increase the price of the shoes, or if they produce more than 3000 shoes, the consumers will not buy all of the shoes. The producers will have a *surplus*—more supply than demand—so they must decrease the price in order to sell all of the shoes. On the other hand, if they make fewer than 3000 shoes, there will be shoe *shortage*—more demand than supply—and the price will go up.

According to the Law of Supply and Demand, the equilibrium price is the best price for the goods. The consumers and the producers will agree on this price because it is the only price that helps them both equally.

Comprehension Questions

Directions: *True or false? Write "T" in the space if the statement is true. Write "F" if it is false.*

_____ 1. People buy more when prices are high.

_____ 2. Producers will make more goods if they can get higher prices for the goods.

_____ 3. The best price for goods is the equilibrium price.

_____ 4. The equilibrium price helps the consumers and the producers equally.

_____ 5. If the producers make the prices of the goods higher than the equilibrium price, the consumers will buy all of the goods.

_____ 6. If there is a shortage of goods, the price of the goods will decrease.

_____ 7. Supply equals demand at the equilibrium point.

_____ 8. If the producers have a surplus of goods, they must increase the price in order to sell all of the goods.

Directions: *Choose the* best *answer.*

1. Why does an increase in price cause an increase in supply?
    a. Consumers buy more goods when prices are high.
    b. Producers make more goods when prices are high.
    c. Producers want to sell all of their goods.
    d. Consumers will not buy all of the goods.

2. Why does a decrease in prices cause an increase in demand?
    a. Consumers buy fewer goods when prices are low.
    b. Producers make fewer goods when prices are low.
    c. Producers make more goods when prices are high.
    d. Consumers buy more goods when prices are low.

3. What do business firms look at when they make decisions about prices and production?
    a. the supply curve
    b. the demand curve
    c. the equilibrium point
    d. all of the above (a, b, and c)

4. Why will consumers and producers agree on the equilibrium price?
    a. It will help them both equally.
    b. It is the only price for the goods.
    c. It is the lowest price.
    d. All of the goods will be sold.

5. When will producers have a surplus of goods?
    a. when supply equals demand
    b. when there is more supply than demand
    c. when there is more demand than supply
    d. when they sell all of their goods

Reading a Graph

Directions: *Figure 6-4 shows the supply and demand curves for pocket calculators at Podunk University. Read the graph and answer the questions.*

1. What is the *equilibrium price* for calculators at Podunk Unviersity, according to Figure 6-4?

_____

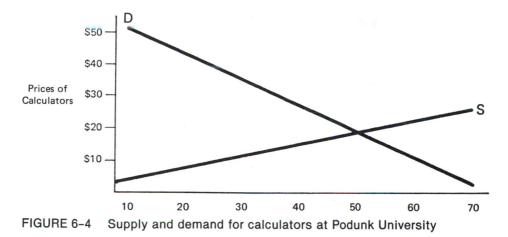

FIGURE 6-4   Supply and demand for calculators at Podunk University

2. How many calculators will the consumers buy at this price?

_____

3. If the producers increase the price of the calculators to $50, how many calculators will the consumers buy?

_____

4. If the producers make 65 calculators, at what price will the consumers buy all of the calculators?

_____

Definitions in Context

Directions: *The author gives definitions for these words in the text. Find the definitions in the text and write them in the spaces.*

1. supply: _____

2. demand: _____

3. surplus: _____

4. shortage: _____

Directions: *What do you think? Answer these questions and discuss your answers with other students in your class.*

1. Why did the author write this text?
   a. to explain the Law of Supply and Demand
   b. to show how prices increase

c. to give general information about economics

d. to answer questions about prices

2. Who did the author write this text for?

a. economists

b. students of economics

c. business firms

d. shopkeepers

3. Does the Law of Supply and Demand explain all changes in the prices of goods? Why or why not?

Rent Control

Photo by Cheri Wilder

Introduction

Supply and demand control the prices of goods, but sometimes governments control prices to help the people. In many countries, the government controls prices of food, clothing, and housing to help poor people who cannot pay high prices for these necessities.

One way governments control the price of housing is rent control. In order to help poor people who cannot pay high rents, the government tells the owners of apartments and houses how much the rent for their apartments and houses should be.

Rent control helps poor people pay their rent, but some economists say that rent control causes housing shortages. According to them, rent controls caused a housing shortage in New York City because these controls pushed the price of housing below the equilibrium price.

What do you think about rent control? This chapter looks at two sides of the rent-control problem: the side of the owners and builders, and the side of the renters. Which side do you think is correct?

Vocabulary Preparation

Vocabulary in Context

Directions: *Read the sentences, guess the meaning of the underlined word or phrase, then answer the question. Please do not use your dictionary.*

1. When they came home from the war, some of the <u>soldiers</u> did not want to talk about the fighting they had done.

   <u>Soldiers</u> are people who _____.
   a. do not like to fight
   b. must fight in wars
   c. like to talk about fighting
   d. do not want to talk about fighting

2. Because of the war, the government <u>imposed</u> a new tax on the people. The people did not want to pay the new tax, but the government said it was necessary.

   When governments <u>impose</u> a tax on their people, the people

   _____.
   a. must pay it
   b. do not pay it
   c. do not want it
   d. vote on it

3. When she tried to pay, the sales clerk did not look at her. When she asked him to help her, he did not talk to her. She was angry because he <u>ignored</u> her.

   To <u>ignore</u> someone is _____.
   a. to look at someone
   b. to talk to someone
   c. not to look at or talk to someone
   d. to ask someone for help

4. David and his friends are <u>worried about</u> the examination. They must get good grades on the exam in order to go to a university. They study very hard, but they are afraid they will not pass the exam. Sometimes they cannot eat or sleep because they are worried about the examination.

   When students are <u>worried about</u> an examination, they

   _____.
   a. are afraid they will not pass it
   b. cannot go to a university
   c. do not study for their exams
   d. get good grades on the exams

5. Americans who rent houses or apartments pay <u>at least</u> 25 percent of their income for rent. Some renters pay more than 50 percent of their income for rent, while others pay as little as 25 percent or 30 percent of their income for rent, but none of them pay less than 25 percent.

   "<u>At least</u> 25 percent of their income" means _____.
   a. less than 25 percent
   b. more than 25 percent
   c. 25 percent or less
   d. 25 percent or more

   Compound Words: A *compound word* consists of two words put together. For example, the word "bedroom" consists of two words: "bed" and "room." A *bedroom* is "a room with a bed."
   Here are some more examples of compound words:

   drugstore = "drug" + "store" (a store that sells drugs)
   policeman = "police" + "man" (a man who works for the police)
   weekend = "week" + "end" (the end of the week)

Directions: *Here are some sentences about compound words. The first sentence in each group is complete. The other sentences are not complete.*

Use the information in the first sentence to help you complete the other sentences.

1. A *shopkeeper* is a person who takes care of a shop (a small store).

2. A *housekeeper* is a person who takes care of a
    _____.

3. A *zookeeper* is a person who takes care of the animals in a
    _____.

4. A *goalkeeper* is a _____ in a soccer game.

5. A *landlord* is a man who rents land, houses, or apartments to other people.

6. A *landlady* is a _____ who rents land, houses, or apartments to other people.

7. A *landowner* is a person who _____.

8. *Income* is money that "comes in" to a person or a group of people, usually for their work.

9. A *low-income* family is a family that has a low
    _____ .

10. *Low-income* housing is houses or apartments for people who have
    _____.

11. A *two-income* family is a family that has _____.

12. A *bedroom* is a room with a bed.

13. A *bathroom* is a room with a _____.

14. A *one-bedroom apartment* is an apartment with
    _____.

15. A *two-bedroom apartment* is an apartment with
    _____.

Text

Rent Control

In most American cities, the rent for a one-bedroom apartment was $250 or more per month in recent years. In some smaller cities such as Louisville, Kentucky or Jacksonville, Florida the rent was less, but in larger cities it was more. For example, if you lived in Los Angeles, you had to pay $400 or more to rent a one-bedroom apartment, and the same apartment rented for $625 and up in Chicago. The most expensive rents in the U.S. were in New York City, where you had to pay at least $700 a month to rent a one-bedroom apartment in most parts of the city.

Renters and city planners are worried about the high cost of renting apartments. Many cities now have rent-control laws to keep the cost of renting low. These laws help low-income families who cannot pay high rents.

Rent control in the United States began in 1943 when the government imposed rent controls on all American cities to help workers and the families of soldiers during World War II. After the war, only one city—New York—continued these World War II controls. Recently, more and more cities have returned to rent controls. At the beginning of the 1980s, nearly one fifth of the people in the United States lived in cities with rent-control laws.

Many cities have rent-control laws, but why are rents so high? Builders and landlords blame rent controls for the high rents. Rents are high because there are not enough apartments to rent, and they blame rent controls for the shortage of apartments. Builders want more money to build more apartment buildings, and landlords want more money to repair their old apartment buildings. But they cannot increase rents to get this money because of the rent-control laws. As a result, landlords are not repairing their old apartments, and builders are not building new apartment buildings to replace the old apartment buildings. Builders are building apartments for high-income families, not low-income families, so low-income families must live in old apartments that are in disrepair. Builders and landlords claim that rent-control laws really hurt low-income families.

Many renters disagree with them. They say that rent control is not the problem. Even without rent controls, builders and landlords will continue to ignore low-income housing because they can make more money from high-income housing. The only answer, they claim, is more rent control and government help for low-income housing.

Comprehension Questions

Directions: *True or false? Write "T" in the space if the statement is true. Write "F" if it is false.*

_____ 1. The rent for a one-bedroom apartment is higher in larger American cities than in smaller ones.

_____ 2. Cities use rent-control laws to keep the cost of renting high.

_____ 3. All American cities had rent control during World War II.

_____ 4. New York City has rent-control laws now.

——— 5. In cities with rent control, builders are building apartments for low-income families.

——— 6. Landlords can get money to repair their old apartment buildings if they can increase rents.

——— 7. Builders and landlords think that rent control helps low-income families.

——— 8. Renters blame rent controls for the high cost of renting apartments.

Directions: *Choose the best answer.*

1. Why did the U.S. government impose rent control on American cities in 1943?
   a. to help low-income families.
   b. to help workers and soldiers' families
   c. to help the families of builders and landlords
   d. to help high-income families

2. When did rent control begin in the United States?
   a. in 1980
   b. during World War II
   c. after World War II
   d. at the beginning of the 1980s

3. Which city had the highest rent for a one-bedroom apartment in 1980?
   a. Jacksonville, Florida
   b. Los Angeles
   c. Chicago
   d. New York

4. According to the builders and landlords, why is there a shortage of apartments in some American cities?
   a. because of rent controls
   b. because there are too many low-income families
   c. because they make more money from high-income housing
   d. because they want to help low-income families

5. According to many renters, why do builders and landlords ignore low-income housing?
   a. because the only answer is more rent control
   b. because the government helps low-income families

c. because they make more money from high-income housing

d. because they want to help low-income families

6. What is the *topic sentence* of paragraph 4 in the text? (*Note:* see Unit 5 Paragraph Study for an explanation of "topic sentence.")

   a. Many cities have rent control, but why are the rents so high?

   b. Builders and landlords blame rent controls for the high rents.

   c. Builders want more money to build new apartment buildings, and landlords want more money to repair their old apartment buildings.

   d. They claim that rent controls really hurt low-income families.

7. What is the *topic* of paragraph 1 in the text? (*Note:* See Unit 1 Paragraph Study for an explanation of "topic.")

   a. the one-bedroom apartments in most American cities

   b. the rent for a one-bedroom apartment in most American cities.

   c. the rent for a one-bedroom apartment in large cities

   d. the most expensive apartments in the United States

Causes and Results: The text tells us about the causes and results of rent control in the United States.

EXAMPLE:

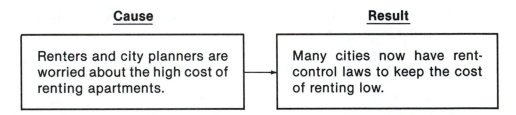

Cause	Result
Renters and city planners are worried about the high cost of renting apartments.	Many cities now have rent-control laws to keep the cost of renting low.

In paragraph 4 of the text, builders and landlords say that high rents are the result of rent controls. In other words:

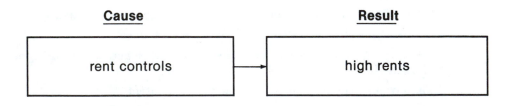

Cause	Result
rent controls	high rents

Directions: *Find the results of these causes in paragraph 4 and write the results in the spaces. The first one is done for you.*

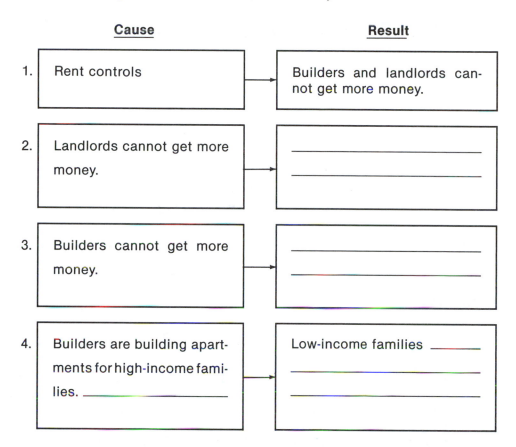

	Cause	Result
1.	Rent controls	Builders and landlords cannot get more money.
2.	Landlords cannot get more money.	_____
3.	Builders cannot get more money.	_____
4.	Builders are building apartments for high-income families. _____	Low-income families _____

Directions: *What do you think? Write answers to the following questions and discuss your answers with other students in your class.*

1. Do rent-control laws really keep the cost of renting low? Why or why not?
2. Do you agree with the builders and landlords who say that rent control really hurts low-income families? Why or why not?
3. Can rent-control laws help low-income families in your country? Why or why not?
4. Does the author of this text think that rent control helps low-income families?

A Perfect Place

Introduction

Some people live in comfortable houses, wear good clothes, eat good food, and make enough money to buy the things they want. Other people do not have comfortable houses or clothes and do not have enough food or money. Why can't everyone be equal? Why do some people live better than others?

Realists say that some people will always be happier than other people. There will always be rich people and poor people because that is the way life really is. Poverty, hunger, disease, crime, and war are all part of life as it really is. Idealists, on the other hand, want to make life better than it is today. They think that we can make the world "a perfect place" if we try to change the way people live.

Idealists all agree that we can make the world a better place, but not all of them agree about how to do it. This chapter is about different ideas for making the world "a perfect place."

Vocabulary Preparation

Vocabulary in Context

Directions: *Read the following newspaper article and guess the meanings of the underlined words. Then answer the questions. Please do* not *use your dictionary.*

PEOPLE FIGHT AGAINST POVERTY, HUNGER, CRIME

Anytown (LP). According to War Against Poverty Director Jack Henderson, the "War" against poverty is not a real war. There are no guns, no soldiers, no armies in this war. People are not fighting against people; they are fight against poverty, hunger, and crime.

Poverty Causes Crime

Poverty is the main enemy in Jack Henderson's war. Many people are poor. They do not have enough money for comfortable housing or clothing. They do not have the personal possessions they want: bicycles, radios, cars, televisions, refrigerators, etc.

Hunger is the result of poverty. Poor people do not have enough money, so they do not have enough food to eat.

"Most crime is the result of poverty and hunger," Henderson claims. When poor people see others with money, food, and personal possessions, they want to have those things too. "A hungry man is an angry man, so a poor man will try to take the things he wants," he explains. Stealing, killing, and other crimes are often the result of poor people trying to get the things they want.

One Society

"Poor people think they are not part of society," Henderson says. "They think that they are alone in the world. We must show them that they are not alone, that we all live together in one society." In order to show poor people that they are part of society, the War Against Poverty begins in the villages, towns, cities, and other communities where poor people live. If they know that they are an important part of the community, poor people will understand that they are also part of the larger society in which we all live.

1. In a *real* war, people fight against _____.
   a. people
   b. poverty
   c. hunger
   d. crime

2. Bicycles, radios, cars, televisions, and refrigerators are examples of

   _____.
   a. poverty
   b. comfortable housing
   c. communities
   d. personal possessions

3. Stealing and killing are examples of _____.
   a. poverty
   b. hunger
   c. crime
   d. society

4. Villages, towns, and cities are examples of _____.
   a. society
   b. communities
   c. important parts
   d. the War Against Poverty

5. Which word is the opposite of *together*? _____
   a. society
   b. community
   c. poor
   d. alone

6. People feel *hunger* when they _____.
   a. do not have enough money
   b. do not have enough food to eat
   c. take the things they want
   d. have personal possessions

7. People are living in *poverty* when they _____.
   a. do not have enough money
   b. do not have enough food to eat
   c. take the things they want
   d. see others with money, food, and personal possessions

8. *Society* consists of _____.
   a. poor people
   b. people with money, food, and personal possessions
   c. people who are alone in the world
   d. all of the people together

   More Vocabulary in Context

Directions: *Read the following groups of sentences and guess the meanings of the underlined words. Then answer the questions. Please do* not *use your dictionary.*

Group 1. At first, Robinson Crusoe did not know where he was. But when he climbed to the top of the highest hill and saw water all around him, he knew he was on an island.

   1. An island is a place of land _____.
      a. at the top of a hill

b. with water all around it

c. where Robinson Crusoe lives

Group 2. Socrates, the ancient Greek philosopher, liked to ask his students questions in order to teach them. Plato, another thinker from ancient Greece, was one of Socrates' students. Plato wrote down the questions and answers of Socrates and his students and called them dialogues, or conversations. Socrates and Plato are famous today because many people read and study these dialogues of Socrates and his students.

2. Which phrase has the same meaning as *ancient Greek philosopher*?
   a. one of his students
   b. dialogues of Socrates and his students
   c. in order to teach them
   d. thinker from ancient Greece

3. Which word has the same meaning as *dialogues*?
   a. questions
   b. answers
   c. conversations
   d. famous

4. When many people know about a person, we can say that the person is

   _____.

   a. famous
   b. a philosopher
   c. a student
   d. ancient

Group 3. Special alkaline batteries last up to five times longer than ordinary zinc-carbon batteries. Ordinary batteries stop working after three or four hours of use, but special alkaline batteries will continue to work for fifteen or twenty hours.

5. When something *lasts*, it _____.
   a. stops working
   b. is special
   c. continues to work
   d. comes at the end

Recognizing Past Forms: Many of the verbs you will read in the text are in the past tense. Most verbs change form when they are in the past tense. The past forms of most verbs have the suffix "-ed" or "-d."

EXAMPLES:

Past Form	Present Form
start*ed*	start
clos*ed*	close

Directions: *Read these sentences and write the* present *forms of the underlined verbs in the spaces. The first one is done for you.*

1. The teacher <u>spelled</u> my name incorrectly.

   (present form: *spell*_____)

2. The Roman Empire <u>lasted</u> for more than 400 years.

   (present form: _____)

3. John and Marsha <u>named</u> their son Michael.

   (present form: _____)

4. Professor Smith <u>described</u> the new machine by drawing a diagram.

   (present form: _____)

5. We <u>tried</u> to answer the question, but it was too difficult.

   (present form: _____)

6. The class <u>ended</u> at ten o'clock.

   (present form: _____)

Some verbs have irregular past forms.

EXAMPLES:

Past Form	Present Form
came	come
began	begin

Directions: *Read the sentences and write the* present *forms of the underlined verbs in the spaces. The first one is done for you.*

7. I <u>bought</u> a new pen at the bookstore.

   (present form: *buy*_____)

8. Plato <u>wrote</u> about his teacher, Socrates.

   (present form: _____)

9. Jack needed money, so he <u>sold</u> his car.

   (present form: _____)

10. Mrs. Jones <u>found</u> a suitcase full of money in her car.

    (present form: _____)

11. David Johnson <u>founded</u> the Johnson Manufacturing Company in 1969.

    (present form: _____)

Note: The verb "found" has a different meaning in the last sentence. Use your dictionary to find the definition of "found" in this sentence. Definition:

_____.

Compound Words: Sometimes a writer puts "every," "no," or "some" together with another word to make a *compound word.* (*Note:* See Unit 6 "Rent Control" Vocabulary Preparation for an explanation of *compound word.*)

EXAMPLES:

*every*where = "every" + "where" = "in all of the places"

*some*one = "some" + "one" = "one of the people"

*no*thing = "no" + "thing" = "none of the things"

Directions: *Read these sentences and write the meanings of the underlined compound words in the spaces. The first one is done for you.*

1. <u>Everyone</u> in our group has a pencil.

   "everyone" = <u>***all of the people***</u>

2. I put my book <u>somewhere</u>, but I can't remember where.

   "somewhere" = _____

3. I looked in all of the classrooms, but my book was <u>nowhere</u> to be found.

   "nowhere" = _____

4. <u>Everything</u> in this shop is very expensive.

   "everything" = _____

5. Please give me <u>something</u> to read.

   "something" = _____

Text

A Perfect Place

Utopia is a perfect place. It is a place without war, hunger, poverty, or crime. It is a place where the people work together and share. There is no money in Utopia because the people do not need money. They do not have personal possessions because everything belongs to everyone. All of the people are equal in Utopia, and the laws are all fair.

Utopia is not a new place. Plato, the ancient Greek philosopher, described a perfect society in his famous dialogue *The Republic*. In Plato's Republic, philosophers were the kings, and every person had a place in the society. In 1516, Sir Thomas More wrote about an island in the Pacific Ocean where everything was perfect. He named the island "Utopia." In 1602, Tommaso Campanella wrote *The City in the Sun* about a perfect community on the island of Ceylon (now Sri Lanka); and in 1872, Samuel Butler wrote a novel about a perfect country which he named "Erewhon." "Utopia" is a Greek word that means "not a place," and "Erewhon" is the English word "nowhere" spelled backwards.

Many people came to the New World to find utopia. The Shakers, a religious group, wanted to live like the first Christians. The Shakers started their first community in New York in 1776. George Rapp, a German farmer, came to the United States in 1804 to start a utopian community. In 1814, Rapp and his followers bought land for their community in Harmony, Indiana, and they made the things they needed with machines. In 1824, they sold the community to Robert Owen, who started the utopian community of New Harmony there. In New Harmony, everthing belonged to everyone and men and women were equal, but New Harmony lasted only two years. Then Francis Wright began Nashoba, a community where white people and black people could live and work together, near Memphis, Tennessee. Nashoba lasted from 1825 to 1830. A group of intellectuals founded Brook Farm, a utopian farming community, in 1841. However, they did not have many farming skills, so the farm closed in 1847. Four years later, Josiah Warren started Modern Times, an anarchist community near New York City. It closed in 1857.

Utopia is a perfect place, but it is not a real place. Most "real" utopias last only a short time. This is because everyone wants to live in utopia, but no one knows how to make it work. As a result, when we say something is "utopian" today, we mean that it is a good idea, but it is not realistic.

Comprehension Questions

Directions: *True or false? Write "T" in the space if the statement is true. Write "F" if it is false.*

——— 1. Utopia is a perfect place.

——— 2. The idea of utopia is new.

——— 3. The City in the Sun and Erewhon were real places.

——— 4. Harmony, Nashoba, and Modern Times were real places.

——— 5. In utopia, all of the people have money.

——— 6. The laws of utopia are all fair.

——— 7. Most utopian communities last a long time.

——— 8. Today, the word "utopian" means "realistic."

Directions: *Choose the* best *answer.*

1. Why are there no personal possessions in utopia?
   a. The people do not need money.
   b. Everything belongs to everyone.
   c. All of the people are equal.
   d. There is no crime in utopia.

2. What was the name of Plato's perfect society?
   a. The Republic   c. City in the Sun
   b. Utopia   d. Erewhon

3. Where was "The City in the Sun"?
   a. in the Pacific Ocean   c. in New York
   b. on the island of Ceylon   d. near Memphis, Tennessee

4. When did Robert Owen buy the Harmony community?
   a. in 1804   c. in 1824
   b. in 1814   d. in 1826

5. When did the New Harmony community end?
   a. in 1826   c. in 1847
   b. in 1830   d. in 1857

6. How long did Nashoba Community last?
   a. two years   c. in 1830
   b. from 1825   d. five years

7. When did Josiah Warren start Modern Times?
   a. in 1847   c. in 1857
   b. in 1851   d. near New York City

8. Why do most "real" utopias last only a short time?

   a. Everyone wants to live in utopia.

   b. It is difficult to find work in utopia.

   c. No one knows where utopia is.

   d. No one knows how to make a perfect society.

Events and Times

Directions: *Here is a list of events from the text. Look for each event in the text and find the time of the event. Write the time of the event in the space. The first one is done for you.*

Event	Time
1. Sir Thomas More's *Utopia*	*1516*
2. The City in the Sun	____
3. The first Shaker community	____
4. George Rapp came to the U.S.	____
5. Francis Wright began Nashoba	____
6. Modern Times closed	____
7. Samuel Butler wrote *Erewhon*	____
8. Brook Farm began	____

Descriptions and Names

Directions: *The text describes several real and imaginary utopian communities. Here is a list of descriptions of some of these communities. Look for the descriptions in the text and find the names of the communities. Write the name of each community beside its description. The first one is done for you.*

Name	Description
1. *Utopia*	An island in the Pacific ocean
2. ____	An anarchist community
3. ____	They wanted to live like the first Christians
4. ____	Founded by a group of intellectuals
5. ____	Every person had a place in the society
6. ____	Black and white people lived and worked together

7. _____   Men and women were equal

8. _____   Used machines to make things

Directions: *What do you think? Write answers to the following questions and discuss your answers with other students in your class.*

1. Why did Sir Thomas More name his island Utopia?

2. Utopian ideas are good ideas which are not realistic. Can you give some examples of utopian ideas? Why are these ideas unrealistic?

3. Plato, Sir Thomas More, Tommaso Campanello, and Samuel Butler described their ideas of utopia. What is *your* idea of utopia?

4. According to the text, everyone wants to live in utopia, but no one knows how to make it work. Do you think people can make utopia work? Why or why not?

Directions: *Just for fun: "Erewhon" is the word "nowhere" spelled backwards. Here are some more words spelled backwards. Match the backwards words with the words they come from by drawing a line between them. Try to match the words in less than one minute. The first two are done for you.*

1. erewhon	ocean
2. tcefrep	place
3. raw	perfect
4. ecalp	nowhere
5. naipotu	crime
6. enoyreve	everyone
7. cilbuper	war
8. laer	real
9. emirc	utopian
10. naeco	republic

Additional Reading

Visitors to the United States enjoy touring the sites of the famous utopian communities of the 1800s. In Massachusetts they visit the Hancock Shaker Village, which was established in 1780. There they can see some of the buildings, tools, and furniture made by the Shakers, and in August they can sit down to a "World's People's Dinner" of tasty Shaker food. In upstate New York they can tour the Mansion House of the Oneida Community. Founded in 1848, the Oneida Community was famous for its "group marriage" (all 300 members of the community married each other), and visitors can see the excellent silverware the members made. Visitors to the Midwestern states of Ohio, Indiana, and Iowa often stop at Zoar Village, New Harmony, and the

Amana Colonies. Zoar Village, a utopian agricultural community on Ohio's Tuscarawas River, was such a tourist attraction in the 1830s that the community built a hotel to accomodate the large number of tourists. New Harmony is located in the southern part of Indiana. Some of the buildings the followers of George Rapp and Robert Owen built are still standing. In the Amana colonies, a group of small religious communities in east central Iowa, life is much the same as it was 100 years ago. The people of the Amana Colonies wear simple black clothing and use horses instead of cars for their transportation. They do not use modern farm machinery, but their farms produce some of the best food in the state.

Comprehension Questions

Directions: *Choose the* best *answer.*

1. Why did the author write this paragraph?
   a. to give general information about utopian communities in the U.S.
   b. to explain the histories of five utopian communities
   c. to encourage tourists to visit the United States
   d. to encourage tourists to visit the utopian communities

2. Where is the Hancock Shaker Village?
   a. in Massachusetts
   b. in upstate New York
   c. on Ohio's Tuscarawas River
   d. in east central Iowa

3. What was the Oneida Community famous for?
   a. its tasty food
   b. its buildings, tools, and furniture
   c. its group marriage and silverware
   d. its simple clothing and horses

4. What is a "tourist attraction"?
   a. a community that has a hotel
   b. a place many tourists come to see
   c. a utopian agricultural community
   d. the states of Ohio, Indiana, and Iowa

5. In the Amana Colonies, why is life much the same as it was 100 years ago?
   a. They are small religious communities.
   b. They are located in east central Iowa.

    c. The people there do not use modern machines.

    d. The people there wear simple black clothing.

6. What is the topic sentence of this paragraph? (*Note:* See Unit 5 Paragraph Study for an explanation of "topic sentence.")

    a. Visitors to the United States enjoy touring the sites of the famous utopian communities of the 1800s.

    b. Visitors to the Midwestern states of Ohio, Indiana, and Iowa often stop at Zoar Village, New Harmony, and the Amana Colonies.

    c. In upstate New York, they can tour the Mansion House of the Oneida Community.

    d. In Massachusetts, they can visit the Hancock Shaker Village, which was established in 1780.

Directions: *Figure 6–5 is a map of the United States. The locations of the five utopian communities in this paragraph are marked on the map, but the names of the communities are missing. Write the missing names in the spaces. You may need a map of the United States to help you. The first one is done for you.*

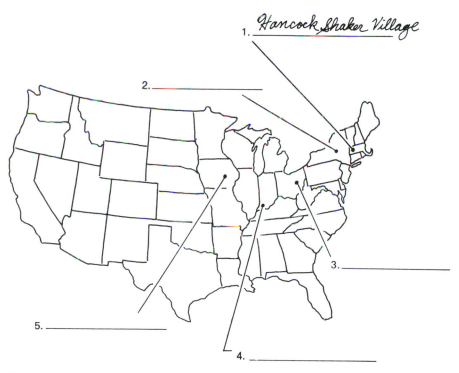

1. *Hancock Shaker Village*

2. _____

3. _____

4. _____

5. _____

FIGURE 6–5 Utopian communities in the U.S.

Directions: *What do you think? Write answers to the following questions and discuss them with other students in your class.*

1. Why do tourists like to visit these utopian communities?

2. Which of these five utopian communities would be the most interesting to visit? Why?

Prereading Questions

Directions: *Try to answer these questions while you are reading the following paragraphs:*

1. Why did young Americans form utopian communities in the 1960s?

2. What was the philosophy of the utopian communities of the 1960s?

3. Who were the leaders of the utopian groups in the 1960s and early 1970s?

In the 1960s, many young Americans were dissatisfied with American society. They wanted to end the Vietnam War and to make all of the people in the U.S. equal. Some of them decided to "drop out" of American society and form their own societies. They formed utopian communities, which they called "communes," where they could follow their philosophy of "do your own thing." A group of artists founded a commune in southern Colorado called "Drop City." Following the ideas of philosopher/architect Buckminster Fuller, they built dome-shaped houses from pieces of old cars. Other groups, such as author Ken Kesey's Merry Pranksters, the followers of San Francisco poet Steve Gaskin, and a group that called itself the Hog Farm, lived in old school buses and traveled around the United States. The Hog Farm became famous when they helped organize the Woodstock Rock Festival in 1969. Steve Gaskin's followers tried to settle down on a farm in Tennessee, but they had to leave when some members of the group were arrested for growing marijuana.

Not all communes believed in the philosophy of "do your own thing," however. Twin Oaks, a commune founded in Virginia in the late 1960s, was baed on the ideas of psychologist B. F. Skinner. The people who lived at Twin Oaks were carefully controlled by Skinner's "conditioning" techniques to do things that were good for the community. In 1972, Italian architect Paolo Soleri began to build Arcosanti, a utopian city in Arizona where 2500 people will live closely together in one large building called an "archology." Soleri believes that people must live closely together so that they will all become one.

Comprehension Questions

Directions: *Choose the* best *answer.*

1. Why did some young Americans decide to "drop out" of society during the 1960s?
   a. They were not satisfied with American society.
   b. They wanted to grow marijuana.
   c. They wanted to go to the Vietnam war.
   d. They did not want all people to be equal.

2. Where did the members of the Hog Farm commune live?
   a. in dome-shaped houses
   b. in old school buses
   c. on a farm in Tennessee
   d. in an archology in Arizona

3. Who gave the people of Drop City the idea to build dome-shaped houses?
   a. Paolo Soleri
   b. B. F. Skinner
   c. Steve Gaskin
   d. Buckminster Fuller

4. What was the Twin Oaks commune based on?
   a. the philosophy of "do your own thing"
   b. Virginia in the late 1960s
   c. the ideas of psychologist B. F. Skinner
   d. the belief that people must live closely together

5. What is an "archology"?
   a. a person who studies archaeology
   b. a large building where people live closely together
   c. a city in Arizona
   d. a technique to control people

Directions: *What do you think? Write answers to the following questions and discuss them with other students in your class.*

1. The young people who decided to "drop out" of American society believed that they could change America by making their own society. Do you think that "dropping out" can change society? Why or why not?

2. The people of Twin Oaks commune were controlled by Skinner's "conditioning" techniques to do things that were good for the community. Why is this different from the philosophy of "do your own thing"?

3. Paolo Soleri believes that people should live closely together so they can all work together like one person. Do you agree with him? Why or why not?

UNIT 7 Reading Skills

WORD STUDY

1. Using Context Clues
2. Recognizing Common Word Stems
3. Finding Appropriate Dictionary Definitions

SENTENCE STUDY

1. Finding the Main Verb in Active and Passive Complex Sentences
2. Identifying Modifying Phrases without Signal Words
3. Simplifying Sentences

PARAGRAPH STUDY

1. Recognizing Paragraph Development Patterns
2. Outlining

READING SPEED

1. Rapid Recognition of Synonymous Sentences
2. Scanning Lists and Tables for Specific Information

Word Study

Using Context Clues

Good readers use context clues to find the meanings of new words as they read. Sometimes the author gives definitions of new words in the context, and sometimes the reader must look for clues in the context in order to guess the meanings of the words.

Exercise 7–1

Directions: *In these sentences, the author uses a synonym or antonym of the underlined word as a context clue. Find the synonym or antonym and write it in the space. The first one is done for you.*

1. I am seldom late for class. My roommate, on the other hand, often arrives five or ten minutes after the class begins.

   seldom ≠ *often* _____

2. The music in the film was dreadful. In fact, it was so bad that I had to leave the theater.

   dreadful = _____

3. East and West Berlin were separated in 1948 when the Soviet Union tried to make Britain, France, and the United States leave Berlin. The two parts of this German city were further divided in 1961 when the East Germans built the Berlin Wall.

   separated = _____

4. Glass is made from silica, which is mostly found in sand, whereas diamond is created from carbon, which is largely found in the form of coal.

   created = _____

   largely = _____

5. If the new agricultural plan succeeds, we will have enough food for all the people in the country. If it fails, however, we will have to import food from other countries.

   fails ≠ _____

6. If you are looking for the latest issue of a magazine in the library, go to the current periodicals shelves. There you will find a pile of all the recent issues of the magazines and the newest issue will be on the top of the pile.

   latest = _____

   current = _____

7. The climate here is so severe that we look forward to every change of season. The beginning of spring marks the end of the cold winter; the beginning of autumn marks the end of the hot summer.

spring ≠ _____

winter ≠ _____

Exercise 7-2

Directions: *In the following sentences, the author uses examples, restatements, or other context clues to explain the meanings of the underlined words. Read the sentences and guess the meanings of the underlined words. Then answer the questions.*

There are three different religious groups in our community. On Friday the Moslems go to the mosque to worship Allah and Mohammed, on Saturday the Jews go to the synagogue to worship Jehovah, and on Sunday the Christians go to the church to worship God and Jesus Christ.

1. When people worship, they _____.

   a. go to a meeting
   b. join a different religious group
   c. become a part of the community
   d. pray according to their religion

The mathematics teacher in our secondary school was very strict. He made rules for the class, and he expected everyone to follow them. For example, if he told students to write all of their answer in pen, he would mark any answer written in pencil wrong—even if it was the correct answer!

2. A strict teacher is a teacher who _____.

   a. works in a secondary school
   b. teaches mathematics
   c. marks answers wrong even if they are correct
   d. wants everyone to follow the rules

3. When the teacher expected everyone to follow his rules, he

   _____.

   a. asked them to follow the rules
   b. wanted them to follow the rules without explanation
   c. told them why they must follow the rules
   d. explained the rules to them

Daily newspapers are written for people who are busy and want to read about the news of the day in a hurry. On weekends, however, people have time to relax, so weekend newspapers—<u>particularly</u> Sunday newspapers—are <u>intended</u> to be read <u>leisurely</u>.

4. "Weekend newspapers—<u>particularly</u> Sunday newspapers" means

   _____.

   a. "Sunday newspapers" is another name for "weekend newspapers."

   b. Sunday newspapers are one important type of weekend newspaper.

   c. Weekend newspapers are an important type of Sunday newspaper.

   d. Weekend newspapers are an important part of Sunday newspapers.

5. What type of person is a Sunday newspaper <u>intended</u> for?

   _____.

   a. A person who is always busy

   b. A person who relaxes on the weekend

   c. A person who is in a hurry

   d. A person who wants to know the news of the day

6. When someone reads a newspaper <u>leisurely</u>, he or she reads it

   _____.

   a. in a relaxed way

   b. in a hurry

   c. very quickly

   d. very slowly

The Emperor always wore the finest clothes in the Empire. He was very <u>proud</u> of his fine clothes, so when some men started advertising a new type of clothes "finer than the Emperor's," he immediately went to see for himself. He asked the men why the new clothes were finer than his, but the men would not tell him. "That is our <u>secret</u>," they said. Finally the Emperor decided to buy all of the new clothes so that he would still have the finest clothes in the Empire. As he walked out of the shop wearing some of the new clothes, a child shouted, "Look! The Emperor isn't wearing any clothes!" Suddenly the Emperor understood the "secret" of his fine new clothes.

7. Which of the following examples shows that the Emperor was <u>proud</u> of his fine clothes?

   a. He always wore the finest clothes in the Empire.

   b. He went to see the new clothes.

    c. He bought all the new clothes so that he would have the finest clothes.

    d. He understood the "secret" of the fine new clothes.

8. A <u>secret</u> is _____.

    a. something that is not true.

    b. something about which people will not tell others

    c. a special type of clothes

    d. a special way of making clothes

    A number of different <u>factors</u> can <u>influence</u> test results. For instance, if the weather is extremely hot or cold, this may cause the test results to be lower, or if the test is given just after lunch or late in the afternoon when the students are tired, the results may be lower than those of a test given early in the morning. On the other hand, higher test results can be obtained when students are alert but relaxed, and in a room which is comfortable and free from distractions.

9. Which of the following <u>factors</u> can cause lower test results?

    a. scheduling the test early in the morning

    b. giving the test in a room without distractions

    c. making sure that students relax before the test

    d. giving the test just after lunch

10. When one thing <u>influences</u> another, it _____.

    a. causes it to change in some way

    b. harms or destroys it

    c. makes it better

    d. causes it to happen

Exercise 7-3

Directions: *Read the following sentences and guess the meanings of the underlined words. Then write a definition for each underlined word in the space. Please do not use your dictionary. The first one is done for you.*

1. The <u>campus</u> of Podunk University is located in the center of Combine, a small town in the agricultural Midwest region. The campus consists of four large classroom buildings, a library building, two dormitories, a sports field, and large areas of grass and trees where students like to walk or sit on warm days.

    campus: *the buildings and land of a university*

2. In addition to the General Assembly, which is the main body of the organization, the United Nations has a number of <u>agencies</u> which it sponsors or controls. These include the International Labor Organization (ILO), the Food and Agriculture Organization (FAO), the United Nation's Educational, Scientific and Cultural Organization (UNESCO), the World Health Organization (WHO), and such economic organizations as the World Bank and the International Monetary Fund (IMF).

agencies: _____

3. The food in that restaurant was so <u>spicy</u> that Jack's eyes filled with tears and he quickly asked the waiter to <u>bring</u> him two glasses of water.

spicy: _____

4. Helen's father works as a <u>guard</u> in the First National Bank. He wears a uniform, carries a gun, and <u>stands</u> at the door to make sure no one tries to steal the money in the bank.

guard: _____

5. Robert Vanderbilt is a solar architect. He <u>designs</u> solar houses. He plans and draws diagrams of different types of houses which can use the heat of the sun to produce heat in the winter, and yet will stay cool in the summer. Twenty years ago no one wanted to build the houses he <u>designed</u>, but today more and more builders are using his plans to build solar houses.

design: _____

6. Sometimes when people are angry they <u>insult</u> each other. For example, when a person ignores a "No Smoking" sign, another person might say, "What's the matter, can't you read?" This person is not really asking a question; he is telling the other person—in an insulting way—not to smoke.

insult: _____

7. People who are very old usually suffer from physical and <u>mental</u> problems. The physical problems include difficulty with seeing, hearing, and walking. The mental problems include difficulty with remembering and difficulty in learning new things.

mental: _____

8. Two men with guns hijacked an airplane and forced the plane to fly to their country. The hijackers said they would <u>release</u> the people on the plane when the government agreed to <u>release</u> their friends from prison. The government agreed to <u>release</u> the <u>prisoners</u>, so the hijackers opened the door of the plane and <u>allowed</u> the people to go out.

release: _____

9. Etymology is the study of the <u>origins</u> of words. Etymologists have found that English words come from many different sources. Sixty percent of the

words in English are from Latin and Greek origins. A large number of English words are from the Germanic languages (including German, Dutch, and the Scandanavian languages) and the Romance languages (French, Spanish, Italian, Portuguese, and Rumanian). A few of the words in modern English have their sources in Arabic, Persian, Hindi, Chinese, Malay, Japanese, and the languages of the American Indians, to name only a few.

origins: _____

Recognizing Common Word Stems

Many of the words in English came from Greek and Latin "stems." A word "stem," or "root" as it is also called, is the basic part of a word without any prefixes or suffixes added. For example, the stem of the word *anonymous* is the Greek word "onyma," which means "name." The prefix "an-" means "without" and the suffix "-ous" tells us that this word is an adjective. Thus we may conclude that *anonymous* is an adjective that means "without a name."

(prefix)		(stem)		(suffix)	
an-	+	-onym-	+	-ous	= anonymous
"without"	+	"name"	+	(adjective)	= an adjective that means "without a name"

Here is a list of common word stems. These are only a few of the many Latin and Greek stems used in English. There are many more, but these are just a few examples.

TABLE 7–1   Some Common Word Stems

Stem	Meaning	Example
-onym-	name	anonymous
-gene-	family	genetics
-vis-, vid-	see	invisible
-audi-	hear	audience
-femin-	woman	feminist
-liber-	free	liberal
-uni-	one	union
-vari-	different, change	variety
-ethni-, -ethno-	race, nation, people	ethnic
-physi-	body, nature	physical
-clude-	close	conclude

Exercise 7–4

Directions: *Use the examples in Table 7–1 to complete the following sentences. The first one is done for you.*

1. A letter without the sender's name on it is a(n)

   _**anonymous**_____ letter.

2. A group of people from the same country or culture is a(n)

   _____ group.

3. When there are many different things to choose from, you have a(n)

   _____ of choices.

4. A(n) _____ is a group of people who come to listen to something.

5. Something we cannot see is _____.

6. When a doctor examines your body it is called a(n)

   _____ examination.

7. Some parents are very _____; they allow their children to do whatever they want.

8. A trade _____ is an organization of different workers who join together to form one large group.

9. We cannot _____ our study until we have all the information.

10. A(n) _____ is a person who believes in women's rights.

11. The study of _____ explains why members of the same family are similar to each other.

It is not necessary to know Greek or Latin to understand the Greek and Latin stems of words in English. Most English dictionaries provide information about the etymologies, or origins, of words. For example, my dictionary gives the following information about the etymology of the word anonymous:

[Gk. *anōnymos an*—without + *onoma, onyma* name]

This information tells us that anonymous comes from the Greek word *anōn-ymos,* which consists of the prefix *an*—meaning "without"—and the stem "*on-oma* or *onyma*" meaning "name."

Now look at this information about the etymology of the word *supervisor* and answer the folowing questions:

[L. *super*— over + *videre* to see]

1. Does the word *supervisor* come from Greek or Latin? _____

2. What is the meaning of the prefix *super*? _____

3. What is the meaning of the stem *videre?* _____

4. Which do you think is the best definition of supervisor?

_____

   a. over to see

   b. a person who looks at things again and again

   c. a person who watches over workers

   d. a special type of television

(*Answers:* 1. Latin   2. over   3. to see   4. c)

Exercise 7–5

Directions: *Each group of three words comes from the same Greek or Latin stem. Look at the etymology and the prefixes and suffixes of the words. Then use the context to find the correct form of the word for each space. The first one is done for you.*

1. **heredity, heritage, inherit**   [L. *hereditare*   heir]

   (*Note:* An *heir* is a person who will get something like land, money, or possessions from his family.)

   Heredity is the way a child gets something from its family; so to <u>inherit</u> something means to get it by heredity, and a person's <u>heritage</u> is all of the things he or she gets from his or her family.

2. **comment, commentary, commentator**   [L. *commentum*   invention]

   When a person *comments* on something, that person is giving his or her opinion about it. A person who gives opinions about sports events is a sports

   _____, and a sports _____ is a statement of opinion about a sports event.

3. **character, characterize, characteristics** [Gk. *charaktēr* stamp, mark]

The *character* of something is the main thing that makes it different from all other things. When we _____ something we show how it is different from other things, and its _____ are the things which make it different.

4. **edit, editor, editorial** [L. *e—* out + *dare* to give]

A newspaper *editor* is a person who takes articles and stories from different writers and puts them together to make the newspaper. The job of an editor is to _____ the newspaper, and when the editor writes an article himself to give his own opinion it is called an

_____.

5. **able, ability, enable** [L. *habilis* suitable]

If you are *able* to do something, it means you can do it. If you have the _____ to drive a car, this will _____ you to use a car for transportation.

Finding Appropriate Dictionary Definitions

When you look up a word in your English dictionary, you may have difficulty finding the word or, once you have found it, you may have difficulty choosing the correct definition of the word.

If you have difficulty finding a word in the dictionary, look for prefixes and suffixes in the word. Dictionaries often list only the simplest form of a word, without prefixes or suffixes, so it may be necessary to find the *stem* of the word in order to find the word in the dictionary.

EXAMPLE:

Look for the word "undisciplined" in your dictionary. You will probably not find this form of the word in your dictionary because it contains a prefix ("un-") and a suffix ("-d"). Instead, you should look for the *stem* of the word ("-discipline-") in order to find it. You know that the prefix "un-" means "not" (see Unit 3 Word Study) and that ("-d") is a suffix which changes a verb to past form (see Unit 4 Vocabulary Preparation for "A Perfect Place"), so the meaning of "undisciplined" will be "not" + the definition of "discipline" as a verb, in the past form.

(prefix)	(stem)	(suffix)
un- "not" +	-discipline- definition of "discipline" as a verb +	-d past form

(*Note:* If you do not know the meaning of a prefix, look it up in your dictionary. Most dictionaries contain definitions of prefixes.)

When you find a word in the dictionary, you will often find more than one definition for the word. In order to choose the correct definition, it is necessary to look for clues in the context. Sometimes the part of speech of the word will lead you to the correct definition (see Unit 5 Word Study). Sometimes it will be necessary to try each definition in the context until you find the best one (see Unit 3 Word Study). Sometimes the context will tell you that the word is used in a particular field (for example, law, medicine, economics). This may help you choose the correct definition.

EXAMPLE:

The judge gave the thief a five year prison *sentence* for stealing from his employer.

My dictionary gives two types of definitions for *"sentence"*: definitions for the field of *grammar* (*Gram.*) and definitions for the field of *law.* Several clues in the context ("judge," "thief," "five years," "prison," "stealing") tell me that "sentence" is used here in the field of law, not the field of grammar. This helps me choose the correct definition of "sentence" for this context.

Exercise 7-6

Directions: *Use your English dictionary to look up the underlined word in each sentence. You will find more than one definition for each word. Use the context to choose the correct definition and write it in the space. The first one is done for you.*

1. The judge <u>sentenced</u> the thief to five years in prison for stealing from his employer.

   sentence = to condemn to punishment

2. For his birthday, she made an <u>elaborate</u> dinner with twenty different kinds of food.

3. The government <u>supplies</u> farmers with information about how to grow more food.

4. Cities offer a wide <u>range</u> of entertainment, from nightclubs and discos to plays and concerts.

5. My sister and I have different <u>tastes</u> in music. She likes Country and Western and disco music; I like <u>jazz</u> and rock music.

6. <u>Discipline</u> is very important in the military. Soldiers must learn to do whatever they are told to do, even if it is wrong.

7. The first page, or front page, of a newspaper is <u>devoted</u> to the most important news of the day.

8. The purpose of the Integrated Studies Department of the University is to find the <u>links</u> between different fields of study and to show students how these <u>fields</u> can work together.

9. When the weather turns cold, deciduous trees lose their leaves and appear to be dead until the <u>spring</u>, when they produce new leaves and start to grow again.

10. After the Minister of Defense was killed by a bomb in his car, the police began <u>arresting</u> everyone who criticized the government.

Sentence Study

Locating the Main Verb in Active and Passive Complex Sentences

Passive Voice

1. Campus newspapers are written by university students.
2. University students write campus newspapers.

These two sentences contain the same information, but they are different in form. Sentence 1 is in *passive voice* and sentence 2 is in *active voice*. The meaning of the two sentences is the same, but the position of the subject and object is different, and the verb in sentence 1 ("are written") has a different form. Writers often use passive sentences when they want to show that the object of the sentence is more important than the subject. In fact, passive sentences often do not contain a subject.

EXAMPLES:

   3. St. Valentine was arrested and put into prison.

   4. (A policeman?) (A soldier?) arrested St. Valentine and put him into prison.

Sentence 3 gives us important information about St. Valentine. We do not know who arrested St. Valentine and put him into prison. Furthermore, the person who arrested him and put him into prison is not important; the important information is that he was arrested (by someone) and put into prison (by someone).

Here are some more examples of passive sentences. Some of these sentences contain a subject and some do not. Which sentences contain subjects? How can you find the subject of a passive sentence?

   5. Daily newspapers are designed to be read quickly.

   6. Sunday newspapers are intended to entertain as well as inform.

   7. A valentine was sent by Charles, Duke of Orleans, to his wife when he was a prisoner in the Tower of London.

   8. Jack was brought up by his father in Trinidad.

   9. More twins must be studied and the results must be carefully compared.

   10. No answer has yet been found to the "heredity vs. environment" question.

(***Answers:*** Sentences 7 and 8 contain subjects. The word "by" comes before the subject of a passive sentence.)

Locating the Main Verb of a Complex Sentence

A good way to find the meaning of a sentence is to look for the main verb of the sentence (see Unit 1 Sentence Study). However, finding the main verb of a complex sentence is often difficult because there is more than one verb in the sentence.

A complex sentence consists of a *main* clause and one or more *modifying* clauses or phrases (see Unit 5 Sentence Study). In order to find the main verb of a complex sentence, first identify the modifying clauses and phrases. The main verb will be the verb which is *not* in one of the modifying clauses or phrases.

EXAMPLE:

In order to determine the extent to which human characteristics are influenced by heredity and environment, James Shields compared identical twins who were brought up together with identical twins who were brought up apart.

The main verb in this sentence is *compared.* The other verbs (*to determine, are influenced,* and *were brought up*) are in modifying clauses or phrases, as shown below:

In order to determine the extent to which human characteristics are determined by heredity and environment, *James Shields compared identical twins* **who were brought up together** *with identical twins* **who were brought up apart.**

boldface = modifying clauses

italic   = main clause

Exercise 7-7

Directions: *Find the main verb in each of the following complex sentences and underline it. (Some of the sentences are in active voice and some are in passive voice.) The first one is done for you.*

1. To keep up with what is happening in the world, people who are well informed <u>read</u> newspapers and news magazines.

2. Most American newspapers also publish a Sunday edition which contains articles about the news of the day and of the week, plus a number of entertainment and advertisement supplements.

3. Other types of newspapers include campus newspapers, which are written by university students, and weekly newspapers, which are intended for specific audiences.

4. People who own home computers can receive their news directly from the wire services, which supply newspapers, magazines, radio, and television with news reports, through special telephone links.

5. On February 14, Americans celebrate St. Valentine's Day, which is a special day for people who are in love.

6. According to one legend, St. Valentine's Day gets its name from a Christian priest named Valentine who lived in Rome during the third century after Christ.

7. There are two types of twins: identical twins, who look exactly the same because they have identical genetic characteristics, and fraternal twins, who have different genetic characteristics.

8. Are thoughts and behavior determined by heredity (the genetic characteristics children inherit from their parents) or by environment (the influences children receive from the world around them)?

9. Some scientists question the results that have come from twin studies because many of the environmental factors are difficult to control.

10. The results of more twin studies must be carefully compared before any real conclusion can be drawn.

Identifying Modifying Phrases without Signal Words

Writers often use *signal words* to identify modifying clauses and phrases (see Unit 5 Sentence Study). However, many modifying phrases are not identified by signal words.

Without signal words, it is often difficult to tell what kind of information these phrases give to the sentence. It is necessary to look at the context in order to understand the kind of information they give.

EXAMPLES:

Directions: *The following paragraph contains a number of modifying phrases without signal words. The modifying phrases have been underlined. Read the paragraph and try to find what kind of information each phrase gives. Then look at the explanation.*

Having finished his homework, Geraldo would often turn on the television. Tired of studying but interested in learning more English, he would watch TV to improve his listening comprehension. Watching the news one night, Geraldo noticed that the man reading the news reports mispronounced the name of the president of Geraldo's country. The news report was about an important meeting to be held in his country, and Geraldo was surprised that a person chosen for the important job of news-reporting did not know how to pronounce the names of all the world's leaders. Geraldo's roommate, a Canadian student who had visited Geraldo's country the year before, said that it was not surprising. "News reporters in your country often mispronounce the name of the Canadian prime minister," he said.

EXPLANATION:

A. Modifying phrases of time:

1) Having finished his homework . . .

This phrase gives us information about the *time* of the information in the sentence. This phrase has the same meaning as the modifying clause *"after he had finished* his homework," so the meaning of the sentence is: *"After he had finished his homework,* Geraldo would often turn on the television."

2) Watching the news one night . . .

This phrase also gives us information about the time of the information in the sentence. This phrase has the same meaning as the modifying clause "*while he was watching* the news one night," so the meaning of the sentence is: "*While he was watching the news one night*, Geraldo noticed that the man reading the news reports mispronounced the name of the president of Geraldo's country."

B. Modifying phrases of cause and purpose:

1) <u>Tired of studying</u> but <u>interested in learning more English</u> . . .

These two phrases give us information about the *cause* of the information in the sentence. These phrases have the same meaning as the modifying clauses "*because he was tired of studying*" and "*because he was interested in learning more English*," so the meaning of the sentence is "*Because he was tired of studying* but *because he was interested in learning more English*, he would watch TV to improve his listening comprehension."

2) . . . <u>to improve his listening comprehension</u>.

This phrase gives us information about the *purpose* of the information in the sentence. This phrase has the same meaning as the phrase "*in order to improve* his listening comprehension," so the meaning of the sentence is: "Tired of studying but interested in improving his English, he would watch TV *in order to improve his listening comprehension.*"

C. Modifying phrases that give information about a noun:

1) . . . <u>reading the news reports</u> . . .

This phrase gives us information about the noun "man" in the sentence. This phrase has the same meaning as the modifying clause "*who was reading the news reports*," so the meaning of this part of the sentence is "The man *who was reading the news reports* mispronounced the name of the president of Geraldo's country."

2) . . . <u>to be held in his country</u> . . .

This phrase gives us information about the noun "meeting" in the sentence. This phrase has the same meaning as the modifying clause "*which was going to be held* in his country," so the meaning of this part of the sentence is: "The news report was about an important meeting *which was going to be held in his country.*"

3) . . . <u>chosen for the important job of news-reporting</u> . . .

This phrase gives us information about the noun "person" in the sentence. This phrase has the same meaning as the modifying clause "*who was chosen* for the important job of news-reporting," so the meaning of this part of the sentence is: "Geraldo was surprised that a person *who was chosen for the important job of news-reporting* did not know how to pronounce the names of all the world's leaders."

4) . . . a Canadian student who had visited Geraldo's country the year before . . .

This phrase gives us information about the noun "roommate" in the sentence. This phrase has the same meaning as the modifying clause "*who was a Canadian student who had visited Geraldo's country the year before*," so the meaning of this sentence is: "Geraldo's roommate, *who was a Canadian student who had visited Geraldo's country the year before,* said that it was not surprising."

Exercise 7-8

Directions: *Look at the following groups of sentences. One sentence has the same meaning as the first sentence in the group. Find the sentence with the same meaning and put a check (✓) beside it. The first one is done for you.*

1. Daily newspapers are designed to be read quickly by busy people looking for specific information.

   _____ a. Daily newspapers are designed to be read quickly by busy people in order to look for specific information.

   _____ b. Daily newspapers are designed to be read quickly by busy people while they are looking for specific information.

   __✓__ c. Daily newspapers are designed to be read quickly by busy people who are looking for specific information.

2. Students learning English in English-speaking countries find the news a useful source of language practice.

   _____ a. Because students are learning English in English-speaking countries, they find the news a useful source of language practice.

   _____ b. Students who are learning English in English-speaking countries find the news a useful source of language practice.

   _____ c. After students have learned English in English-speaking countries, they find the news a convenient source of language practice.

3. Oscar and Jack are identical twins, separated when they were babies by their parents' divorce.

_____ a. Oscar and Jack are identical twins who were separated when they were babies by their parents' divorce

_____ b. Oscar and Jack are identical twins because they were separated when they were babies by their parents' divorce.

_____ c. Oscar and Jack are identical twins after they had been separated when they were babies by their parents' divorce.

4. In 1962, James Shields compared identical twins brought up together with identical twins brought up apart.

_____ a. In 1962, James Shields compared identical twins after they were brought up together with identical twins after they were brought up apart.

_____ b. In 1962, James Shields compared identical twins while they were brought up together with identical twins while they were brought up apart.

_____ c. In 1962, James Shields compared identical twins who were brought up together with identical twins who were brought up apart.

5. To keep up with what is happening in the world, well-informed people read newspapers and news magazines.

_____ a. After they have kept up with what is happening in the world, well-informed people read newspapers and news magazines.

_____ b. Because they keep up with what is happening in the world, well-informed people read newspapers and news magazines.

_____ c. People who are well-informed read newspapers and news magazines so that they can keep up with what is happening in the world.

6. Considering the number of ethnic groups that make up the U.S. population, it is not surprising that Americans have a variety of holidays.

_____ a. When we consider the number of ethnic groups that make up the U.S. population, it is not surprising that Americans have a variety of holidays.

_____ b. Because we consider the number of ethnic groups that make up the U.S. population, it is not surprising that Americans have a variety of holidays.

_____ c. In order to consider the number of ethnic groups that make up the U.S. population, it is not surprising that Americans have a variety of holidays.

7. On Halloween, children dressed like ghosts and witches go from house to house shouting "Trick or treat!"

_____ a. On Halloween, because children are dressed like ghosts and witches, they go from house to house when they shout "Trick or treat!"

_____ b. On Halloween, children who are dressed like ghosts and witches go from house to house while they shout "Trick or treat!"

_____ c. On Halloween, after they are dressed like ghosts and witches, children go from house to house because they are shouting "Trick or treat!"

8. Never having heard of valentines before, Geraldo was surprised to receive one from his girlfriend on February 14.

_____ a. Because he had never heard of valentines before, Geraldo was surprised to receive one from his girlfriend on February 14.

_____ b. After he had never heard of valentines before, Geraldo was surprised to receive one from his girlfriend on February 14.

_____ c. In order to never hear of valentines before, Geraldo was surprised to receive one from his girlfriend on February 14.

Simplifying Sentences

Long sentences are often more difficult to understand than short sentences. However, if you can simplify a long sentence by dividing it into two or more short sentences, it may be easier to understand.

EXAMPLE:

Most American newspapers publish an enlarged Sunday edition containing articles about the news of the day and of the week, plus a number of entertainment and advertising supplements.

This sentence can be divided into three shorter sentences:

1) Most American newspapers publish an enlarged Sunday edition.

2) This Sunday edition contains articles about the news of the day and of the week.

3) This Sunday edition contains a number of entertainment and advertising supplements.

Exercise 7-9

Directions: *Simplify the following sentences by dividing them into two or more shorter sentences. The first one is done for you.*

1. Owners of home computers can receive their news directly from the wire services—news agencies which supply newspapers, magazines, radio, and television with news reports—through special telephone links.

   1) *Owners of home computers can receive their news directly from the wire services through special telephone links.*

   2) *Wire services are news agencies which supply newspapers, magazines, radio, and television with news reports.*

2. The origins of this holiday are uncertain, but according to one legend it gets its name from a Christian priest named Valentine who lived in Rome during the third century after Christ.

   1) _____

   2) _____

   _____

   3) _____

   4) _____

   _____

3. There are two types of twins: identical twins, who look exactly the same because they have identical genetic characteristics, and fraternal twins, who have different genetic characteristics.

   1) _____

   _____

   2) _____

   _____

   3) _____

4. Oscar and Jack are identical twins, separated when they were babies by their parents' divorce.

   1) _____

2) _____

_____

5. Are thoughts and behavior determined by heredity (the genetic characteristics children inherit from their parents) or by environment (the influences children receive from the world around them)?

1) _____

_____

2) _____

_____

3) _____

_____

Paragraph Study

Recognizing Paragraph Development Patterns

Every paragraph has a topic and a main idea (see Unit 3 Paragraph
Study). Many paragraphs have topic sentences (see Unit 5 Paragraph Study).
The topic sentence is often the first sentence in the paragraph, but it can also
be at the end or in the middle of the paragraph. Sometimes the topic sentence
is really two sentences in different parts of the paragraph, and some paragraphs do not have topic sentences.

Paragraphs that begin with the topic sentence are often used when the
writer wants to make a general statement about the topic and then give specific details, examples, or reasons to show that the general statement is true.

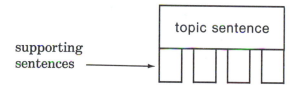

EXAMPLE:

Newspapers can provide more news than radio or television. Re-
stricted in the amount of time available for news reporting, radio and
television news programs can give only a limited amount of information

about each news event. Newspapers, on the other hand, are limited only by the amount of space available for each news article, so each article tends to contain more information than a radio or television news story. This is largely because of the difference in speed between reading silently and reading aloud. Most people can read a news story silently more quickly than they can read it aloud. Consequently, a person reading a newspaper for thirty minutes can receive more information than a person listening to a radio or television news program for thirty minutes.

The writer's general statement is that the newspapers provide more news than radio and television. He gives three specific reasons to show that this statement is true:

TOPIC SENTENCE:	Newspapers provide more news than radio and television.

REASONS:	restricted amount of time for radio and TV news	newspaper articles contain more information about each news event	silent reading faster than reading aloud

Paragraphs that end with the topic sentence are used when the writer wants the reader to look at the information first, and then to draw a conclusion. This kind of paragraph is particularly useful for reporting an experiment or for surprising the reader.

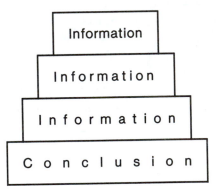

EXAMPLE:

Shields observed that identical twins were more similar in height, weight, and intelligence than fraternal twins. This supported the hypothesis that heredity determines such characteristics. However, he further observed that identical twins brought up together were more similar than identical twins brought up apart. This led him to conclude that, although heredity plays an important part in determining size and intelligence, environment is also an important factor.

The writer's (and the experimenter's) conclusion is expressed in the last sentence. However, the writer wants the reader to look at all the information before coming to the conclusion.

> Identical twins are more similar than fraternal twins.
>
> Identical twins brought up together are more similar than identical twins brought up apart.
>
> Although heredity plays a part in determining size and intelligence, environment is also an important factor.

When a writer wants to develop an idea in two different ways, paragraphs in which the topic sentence is in the middle, or in which the topic sentence is really two sentences in different parts of the paragraph, are used.

When the topic sentence is in the middle, the paragraph usually begins with information that leads the reader to a general statement (the topic sentence); it then gives more information to support the general information.

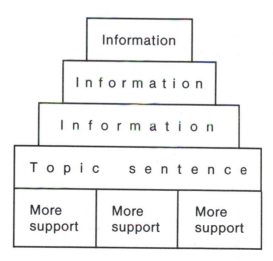

EXAMPLE:

Americans observe the traditional Christian holidays of Easter (after the beginning of spring) and Christmas (on December 25). In addition, they celebrate traditional American holidays such as Independence Day on the Fourth of July, and Thanksgiving on the fourth Thursday in November. In addition to these traditional holidays, Americans also observe some less famous holidays which are rather unusual. On Groundhog Day, February 2, an animal decides when winter will end. On April Fool's Day, April 1, people play tricks on one another. Children try to frighten everyone on Halloween, October 31, and on the first Saturday after November 11, girls chase boys in the Sadie Hawkins' day race.

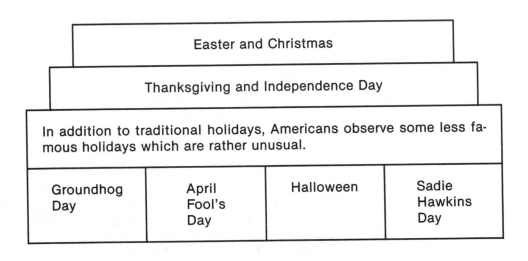

When the topic sentence is really two sentences, the first sentence is usually at the beginning of the paragraph, followed by supporting information. The second sentence is often in the middle of the paragraph, followed by its own supporting information.

Topic sentence Part 1		
support	support	support
Topic sentence Part 2		
support	support	support

EXAMPLE:

Oscar and Jack are identical twins, separated when they were babies by their parents' divorce. Jack was brought up by their Jewish father in Trinidad, but his brother Oscar went to live with their mother's family in Czechoslovakia. In fact, Oscar did not know he was Jewish until Jack found him in Germany in 1954. Jack is proud to be a Jew, but Oscar still does not like to talk about his Jewish heritage. Yet the twins are similar in many ways. They both like spicy food and sweet drinks. In school they both did well in sports but poorly in mathematics. They share some of the same idiosyncracies as well, such as flushing the toilet before and after using it.

TOPIC SENTENCE PART 1:

> Oscar and Jack are identical twins, separated when they were babies by their parents' divorce.

Jack → father in Trinidad Oscar → mother's family in Czechoslovakia	Oscar did not know he was Jewish until Jack told him.	Jack: proud to be a Jew Oscar: does not like to talk about it.

TOPIC SENTENCE PART 2:

> Yet the twins are similar in many ways.

Like spicy food and sweet drinks	Did well in sports but not in math	Flush the toilet before and after using it

Sometimes, however, the second sentence is at the end of the paragraph:

Topic sentence Part 1		
support	support	support

information

information

Topic sentence Part 2

EXAMPLE:

Students learning English in English-speaking countries find the news a useful source of language practice. To improve their listening comprehension, they listen to the news on the radio and watch it on television. Then they check their comprehension by reading newspapers and news magazines. Everyone likes to talk about the news. In the office, on campus, at parties, or on the street, conversations often begin with questions like "What's new?", "What's happening?", or "Have you heard about ...?" By staying well-informed, these students find it easier to enter into conversations about the news.

TOPIC
SENTENCE
PART 1:

> Students learning English find the news a useful source of language practice.

| listen to it on the radio | watch it on television | read newspapers and news magazines |

Everyone likes to talk about the news.

Conversations often begin with questions about the news.

PART 2:

By staying well informed, these students find it easier to enter into conversations about the news.

Paragraphs without topic sentences are used when a writer only wants to link together a series of events or ideas. These paragraphs often support the information given in other paragraphs in the text.

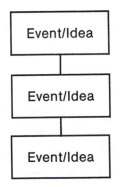

Event/Idea

Event/Idea

Event/Idea

EXAMPLE:

The next valentine was sent by Charles, Duke of Orleans, to his wife in 1415 A.D. while he was a prisoner in the Tower of London. His valentine is now on exhibit in the British Museum. The first commercially printed valentines did not appear until 1809. Some of these valentines were not messages of love. Comic valentines, or "penny dreadfuls" as they were called, were often funny and sometimes insulting. The "Golden Age" of valentines started in the 1840s when valentine-makers began making elaborate and expensive valentines. Jonathan King became famous as a publisher of beautiful and unusual valentines in Britain in the 1870s. Esther Howland was the first to publish valentines in the United States, in the 1860s. She created handmade designs for valentines which cost as much as thirty dollars.

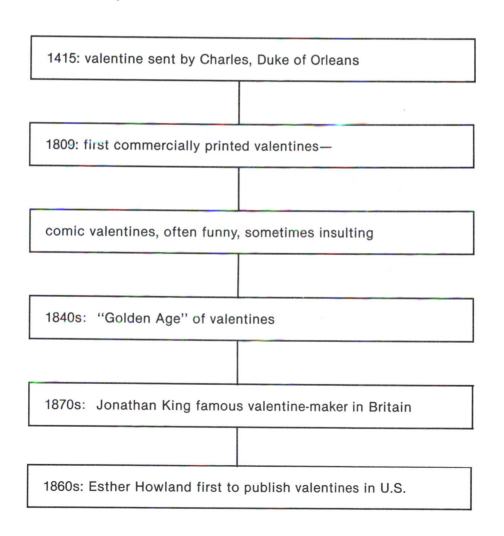

1415: valentine sent by Charles, Duke of Orleans

1809: first commercially printed valentines—

comic valentines, often funny, sometimes insulting

1840s: "Golden Age" of valentines

1870s: Jonathan King famous valentine-maker in Britain

1860s: Esther Howland first to publish valentines in U.S.

Exercise 7-10

Directions: *Read each paragraph and underline the topic sentence. (The topic sentence may be at the beginning, at the end, in the middle, or in two different sentences in the paragraph, or the paragraph may not have a topic sentence.) Then make a diagram of the information in the paragraph. The first one is done for you. When you finish, compare your diagrams with those of other students in your class.*

1.   After one year, the Emperor offered to release Valentine from prison if he would agree to stop performing marriages. Valentine refused, so the Emperor sentenced him to death. Before he was killed, St. Valentine sent a love letter to the daughter of the prison guard. He signed the letter "from your Valentine." <u>That was the first valentine.</u>

Emperor offered to release Valentine after one year if he would stop performing marriages.
Valentine refused—sentenced to death.
Valentine sent a letter to the daughter of the guard.
Valentine signed the letter "from your Valentine."

TOPIC SENTENCE: That was the first valentine.

2.   On February 14 Americans celebrate another unusual holiday, St. Valentine's Day, a special day for lovers. Valentines are cards—usually red and shaped like hearts—with message of love written on them. Lovers send these cards to each other, often anonymously, on St. Valentine's Day.

3.   Jack grew up in Trinidad, an island in the Carribean Sea. As a boy, he went to the synagogue, studied Hebrew, and learned to be a good Jew. He hated Nazis and cheered when the British beat the Germans in the war movies he loved to watch. When he was seventeen years old, he went to Israel to work on a kibbutz. Now he owns an appliance store in California. He works long hours and seldom takes a vacation. His political ideas are somewhat liberal and he accepts the feminist movement.

4.   While reading a newspaper, most people look first at the headline of each article to find out what the article is about. Every newspaper article begins with a headline. The headline is a short title which identifies the topic and main idea of the article. The "byline" is located just under the headline. The byline gets its name from the preposition "by," which is often used to introduce the name of the author of the article. Some bylines do not include the preposition "by" and the author's name. They contain only the name of the organization the article came from. Whether it contains an author's name or the name of an organization, the byline identifies the source of the article.

5.   The most important news of the day is usually on the front page of the newspaper. The rest of the news is usually located in special sections of the newspaper devoted to local, regional, national, international, business, sports, and other news. Efficient newspaper readers know not only where to look for the important news in a newspaper but also how to decide which articles are most important for them to read. By quickly scanning the headlines, they get a general idea of which articles are more important than others. With this information they can decide which articles to read carefully, which articles to read quickly, and which articles not to read at all.

Outlining

Writers often *outline* their ideas before they write. An outline is a plan that lists the topics and subtopics the writer wants to include in the text. The outline also shows how the information will be divided—according to level of generality, time, place, causal relationship, and so on.

Students often write outlines when they study. By outlining the information in a textbook or an article, they can see how the writer organized the information; and an outline is useful for studying before an exam.

EXAMPLE:

Here is a text about a traditional American holiday, Thanksgiving, followed by an outline of the text. Notice how the ideas in the text are arranged in the outline.

Thanksgiving is the day on which Americans thank God for the many good things he has given them. It is a feast day observed on the fourth Thursday in November, about the time most crops are harvested in North America. American families get together on this day to give thanks to God, to eat, and to remember the first Thanksgiving, which took place long ago.

The Pilgrims were a religious group who moved from England to America in the early seventeenth century. Their first year in America was very difficult. Many of the Pilgrims died because they did not have enough food and the winter was very cold. Their next year was much easier. They built strong houses to keep out the cold, and they were able to grow more than enough food. To thank God for their good year, they organized a feast for all of the Pilgrims. They also invited some of the Indians who had helped them learn to hunt and grow food. That was the first Thanksgiving.

Today, Thanksgiving is a family holiday. Family members sometimes travel thousands of miles to be together for Thanksgiving. Traditionally, the women of the family cook a huge dinner of turkey and dressing, sweet potatoes, and pumpkin pie. Everyone is expected to eat as much as possible, and after dinner they sit in the living room holding their stomachs and complaining that they ate too much!

I. Thanksgiving—day on which Americans thank God for giving good things

   A. Feast day

   B. Fourth Thursday in November

      1. about the time most crops are harvested in North America

   C. Families get together

      1. to give thanks to God

      2. to eat

      3. to remember the first Thanksgiving

II. The first Thanksgiving

  A. Pilgrims

    1. religious group

    2. moved from England to America in early 17th century

  B. First year in America was very difficult

    1. not enough food

    2. winter very cold

  C. Next year much easier

    1. built strong houses to keep out cold

    2. able to grow more than enough food

  D. Organized a feast to thank God

    1. invited all Pilgrims

    2. also invited Indians who had helped them

III. Today, Thanksgiving is a family holiday.

  A. Family members travel 1000s of miles to be together

  B. Women of family cook huge dinner

    1. turkey and dressing

    2. sweet potatoes

    3. pumpkin pie

    4. everyone expected to eat as much as possible

  C. After dinner, sit in living room

    1. hold stomachs

    2. complain they ate too much

Exercise 7-11

Directions: *Read the following texts. Then complete the outline for each text by filling in the spaces with information from the text.*

1. In 1862, French troops were sent by Emperor Napoleon III to establish a French colony in Mexico. At that time, Mexico was an independent country under the liberal government of Benito Juarez. The French troops landed on the coast of Mexico and started marching to the capital city, but they were stopped by Mexican troops at the town of Puebla de los Angeles.

    The French attacked the town on May 5, 1862, but the Mexican defenders led by General Zaragoza beat back the attack. Finally, after almost 1000 French soldiers had been killed, the French retreated to the sea. The people of Puebla were so thankful to the defenders that they renamed the town Puebla de Zaragoza in honor of the General's May 5 victory.

Less than a year later, the French returned and captured the town. It remained under French rule until 1867, when General Porfirio Diaz liberated Puebla, but it was the May 5 battle that people remembered as a great victory. Therefore, Cinco de Mayo (the fifth of May) became a national holiday for celebrating Mexico's victory over foreign invaders.

I. _____

_____

   A. Mexico was an independent country under Benito Juarez

   B. French landed on Mexican coast, marched to capital

   C. stopped by Mexican troops at Puebla de los Angeles

II. French attacked the town on May 5

   A. _____

      1. 1000 French soldiers killed

      2. French retreated to the sea

   B. _____

_____

III. _____

   A. Less than a year later, the French captured the town

   B. 1867: Puebla liberated

   C. People remembered the May 5 battle as a great victory

2. When we think of twins, we usually think of identical twins. Identical twins are born together, they are of the same sex, and they look exactly the same. In fact, they look so much the same that people often have difficulty telling them apart.

However, not all twins are identical twins. Fraternal twins, like identical twins, are born together, but they are not always of the same sex and they do not look exactly the same. Sometimes the only way to tell fraternal twins from other brothers and sisters is to find out their birth dates.

Identical twins look exactly the same because they are formed from the same egg, or *zygote*. Thus, identical twins are also known as *monozygotic* twins (*mono* = one, *zygote* = egg). Because they are formed from the same egg, monozygotic twins have the same genetic characteristics. Fraternal twins, on the other hand, are formed from separate eggs, so they are called *dizygotic* twins (*di-* = two). They come from different eggs, so their genetic characteristics are different.

Because they did not understand how twins are formed, people in the past were afraid of twins. In some societies, twin babies were killed or left for wild animals to eat. According to one legend, the city of Rome was founded by twin brothers who were left to die but were brought up by a wolf. Today, the fear of twins is gone, but people are still interested in them. Scientists are particularly interested in studying twins. They hope to find out more about genetics and heredity from twin studies.

  I. Identical twins
     A. born together
     B. same sex
     C. look exactly the same
        1. people often have difficulty telling them apart

 II. _____
     A. _____
     B. _____
     C. _____
        1. birth dates sometimes only way to tell them from other brothers and sisters

III. Identical twins also known as monozygotic twins
     A. formed from same _____
     B. have same _____

 IV. Fraternal twins called _____
     A. formed from _____
     B. _____

  V. _____
      _____
     A. people in the past afraid of twins
        1. _____
        2. _____
        3. _____
     B. scientists are particularly interested in studying twins
        1. _____

   3. Gregor Mendel, a monk who lived in Czechoslovakia in the nineteenth century, was the father of modern genetics. Interested in plant breeding, he performed experiments with peas in the garden of the monastery where he lived. He wanted to find a mathematical formula for the results of plant breeding; instead, he discovered some of the basic rules of genetics.

In 1866 Mendel published an article, "Experiments in Plant Hybrids," in which he presented the rules known today as Mendel's Laws. In order to explain the unusual way in which his peas inherited certain characteristics, he talked about pairs of "elements" (now called "genes") and "antagonistic factors" (now called "alleles"). Not only did these "elements" and "factors" explain the inheritance of pea characteristics, they also opened the door for modern research with genes, chromosomes, and DNA.

Few scientists were interested in Mendel's hypothesis when his article was published. It was not until years later that the world recognized the importance of Mendel's ideas. By that time the monk had become leader of his monastery and was too busy to continue his experiments. Consequently, the father of genetics probably died without knowing how his work had changed the course of science.

I. Gregor Mendel was the father of modern genetics

    A. _____

    B. _____

    C. _____

    D. _____

    E. _____

II. "Experiments in Plant Hybrids" (1866)—Mendel's Laws

    A. To explain how peas inherited characteristics, he talked about

        1. _____

        2. _____

    B. These "elements" and "factors" are

        1. _____

        2. _____

III. _____

    _____

    A. few scientists interested in Mendel's hypothesis in 1866

    B. _____

    _____

    C. _____

    _____

Reading Speed

Rapid Recognition of Synonymous Sentences

In the Sentence Study exercises in this book, you have learned to recognize synonymous sentences—sentences with the same meaning. Recognizing synonymous sentences is important when you are studying from two or more textbooks. Different authors often say the same thing in different words, so it is important to be able to recognize synonymous sentences so that you will know when the authors agree and when they disagree. This exercise will give you practice in recognizing synonymous sentences quickly when you study.

Exercise 7-12

Directions: *Look at the following groups of sentences. One sentence has the same meaning as the first sentence in the group. Find the sentence with the same meaning and put a check (✔) beside it. Try to do this exercise as quickly as you can. The first one is done for you.*

1. Thanksgiving is a feast day observed on the fourth Thursday in November, about the time most crops are harvested in North America.

    _____ a. The fourth Thursday in November observes Thanksgiving as a feast day after most crops in North America are harvested.

    __✔__ b. Americans observe Thanksgiving, a feast day, on the fourth Thursday in November, when North American farmers have harvested most of their crops.

    _____ c. Thanksgiving, which is a feast day, is observed on the fourth Thursday in November while most crops in North America are harvesting.

2. To thank God for their good year, the Pilgrims organized a feast for everyone.

    _____ a. The Pilgrims organized a feast for everyone so that they could thank God for their good year.

    _____ b. In order to ask God for another good year, the Pilgrims organized a feast for everyone.

    _____ c. A feast for everyone organized the Pilgrims to thank God for their good year.

3. In 1862, French troops were sent by Emperor Napoleon III to establish a French colony in Mexico.

   _____ a. Emperor Napoleon III established a French colony in Mexico with French troops in 1862.

   _____ b. A French colony in Mexico was established by French troops sent by Emperor Napoleon III in 1862.

   _____ c. In order to establish a French colony, Emperor Napoleon III sent French troops to Mexico in 1862.

4. Puebla remained under French rule until 1867, when it was liberated by General Porfirio Diaz.

   _____ a. Puebla was liberated by General Porfirio Diaz when it remained under French rule until 1867.

   _____ b. Puebla remained under French rule until General Porfirio Diaz liberated it in 1867.

   _____ c. Puebla was liberated by General Porfirio Diaz until 1867, when it remained under French rule.

5. Identical twins look the same because they are formed from the same egg, or *zygote.*

   _____ a. Because identical twins look the same, they form the same egg, or *zygote.*

   _____ b. Because some eggs, or *zygotes,* form them, identical twins look the same.

   _____ c. Because they are formed from the same *zygote,* identical twins look the same.

6. Interested in plant breeding, Mendel performed experiments with peas in the garden of the monastery where he lived.

   _____ a. Mendel performed experiments with peas in the garden of the monastery where he lived because plant breeding interested him.

   _____ b. Mendel performed experiments with peas in the garden where he lived in the monastery in order to interest himself in plant breeding.

   _____ c. Mendel performed experiments with peas living in the garden of the monastery while he was interested in plant breeding.

7. A newspaper article is introduced by the headline, followed by the byline indicating the source of the article.

———— a. The headline introduces a newspaper article and follows the byline which indicates the source of the article.

———— b. The headline introduces a newspaper article, follows the byline, and indicates the source of the article.

———— c. The headline introduces a newspaper article, and the byline, which indicates the source of the article, follows the headline.

8. Not knowing the importance his ideas were to have for modern genetics, Mendel discontinued his plant breeding experiments.

———— a. Mendel discontinued his plant breeding experiments because he did not know the influence his ideas were going to have on modern genetics.

———— b. Mendel discontinued his plant breeding experiments in order to know the importance of his ideas for modern genetics.

———— c. Mendel discontinued his plant breeding experiments when he did not know how to show the importance of his ideas for modern genetics.

9. Not having grown enough food to last through the cold winter, many Pilgrims died during their first year in America.

———— a. Many Pilgrims died during their first year in America while they did not grow enough food to last through the cold winter.

———— b. Many Pilgrims died during their first year in America after they had not grown enough food to last through the cold winter.

———— c. Many Pilgrims died during their first year in America because they had not grown enough food to last through the cold winter.

10. We cannot draw conclusions from these results alone; more twins must be studied and the results carefully considered before any real conclusions can be drawn.

———— a. Before we can draw any real conclusions, we must study more twins and consider the results carefully.

———— b. We cannot draw any real conclusions because more twins will be studied and the results will be carefully considered.

———— c. We must study more twins and consider the results more carefully because no real conclusions can be drawn.

Scanning Lists and Tables for Specific Information

Scanning is a very important reading skill. When you scan, you look very quickly at a list or table to find some specific information. When you find the information, you stop scanning and read the information. Whenever you look up a word in the dictionary or look for a telephone number in the telephone directory, you are scanning for specific information. Scanning is also useful when you are using a timetable or a schedule, or when you are looking up page numbers in a table of contents or an index.

Exercise 7-13

Directions: *Scan the calendar from the* Colorado Daily *(a campus newspaper) (Figure 7–1) to find the answers to the following questions. Write the answers in the spaces. Try to do this exercise as quickly as possible.*

1. When will the Boulder Portable Computer Club hold its regular club meeting?

_____

2. Where can you go if you want to dance to great music on a big dance floor?

_____

weekend, august 12-13, 1983 · the colorado daily · page 4

What's Happening

For our readers' convenience, listings in this column run from noon to noon. Material must be submitted by noon the day before publication (noon two days beforehand for morning events; noon Friday for Monday's newspaper). Information, including event title, sponsor, time, place and admission charge (if any) should be sent to the *Colorado Daily*, P.O. Box 1719, Boulder, CO 80306 or brought to our offices, Suite 408 in the University Memorial Center, Euclid and Broadway.

FRIDAY, AUGUST 12

NORTHERN COLORADO FENCERS Club meets at 7 p.m. every Friday at Farentinos' Aerobics, Table Mesa Shopping Center. Instruction is available. For information call Gary Copeland, 443-1076.

CONSUMER NETWORK SYSTEM, a growing network of people supporting each other systematically to achieve primary financial freedom, offers a forum every Friday at 7:30 p.m. at Moore & Co. Realty, southeast corner of 30th and Arapahoe. For information call 443-0895.

STAR GAZING sessions begin at 9 and 10 p.m. (weather permitting) at Sommers-Bausch Observatory. Free. Call 492-8915 for reservations.

A CHANCE TO DANCE to great music on a big dance floor, with mirrors, rollerskating, refreshments and no smoking is yours from 9 p.m. to 12:30 a.m. every Friday at Kakes Studios, 2115 Pearl St., in the alley next to Lifestyles. $2 general admission, 50 cents for young people and free for 5 years and under.

SATURDAY, AUGUST 13

GRASSLAND ECOLOGY WALK at the Dunn II Open Space will be led by Park Ranger Brian Peck from 8 to 10 a.m. Bring water, sunhats, and if you have them, binoculars and hand lenses. Meet at the parking lot at the south end of the Mesa Trail, just east of Eldorado Springs.

VOLLEYBALL on a drop-in basis is available on Saturday and Sunday mornings at the North and South Boulder Recreation Centers. For information call 441-3444 or 441-3448.

COLORADO OWNER-BUILDER CENTER is offering a seminar on "Adobe/Rammed Earth: Building With Earth" from 10 a.m. to 5 p.m. at the Boulder Child Care Support Center, 2160 Spruce St. $40 at the door, $35 in advance. For information call Maureen McIntyre, 449-6126.

PALMER DRUG ABUSE PROGRAM holds a young-people-only meeting every Saturday at 11 a.m. at First Christian Church, 950 28th St. Free. For information call Steve Weaver, senior counselor, 449-9622.

AUTHOR WILLIAM BURROUGHS will lead a writers' workshop today and Sunday from 11 a.m. to 1 p.m. at Naropa Institute 2130 Arapahoe Ave. $35. Advance registration is not required, but will be accepted. For information call 444-0202.

HANDWRITING ANALYSIS by Devon will be available from 12:30 to 3 p.m. at Brillig Works Bookstore, 1322 College Ave. $5.

1983 JEFFERSON COUNTY FAIR AND RODEO will feature a large draft horse pulling contest at 2 p.m. at the Jefferson County Fairgrounds, West 6th Avenue and Indiana in Golden. Free. For information call 238-6431.

SUNDAY, AUGUST 14

LIVING WATERS CHRISTIAN FELLOWSHIP holds a worship service every Sunday at 10:30 a.m. in Duane Physics G-030.

CENTER FOR NEW WORLD THOUGHT offers a group activity class titled "Open Your Heart to the Spirit Within" every Sunday from 11 a.m. to 1 p.m. at 1240 Pine St. $3 per class. For information call 440-9680.

BOULDER PORTABLE COMPUTER CLUB is offering a variety of classes today between 11 a.m. and 10:30 p.m. and will hold their regular club meeting (free) from 5 to 7:30 p.m. All classes and meeting are held at 717 19th St. For information call 447-8833.

GANGES TO THE NILE, a global cultural journey that celebrates and explores the rich musical, poetic and literary traditions of the peoples of the world, is broadcast every Sunday from 12:30 to 3 p.m. on public radio station KGNU, 88.5 FM. The program is produced and hosted by David Barsamian.

BOULDER ECKANKAR CENTER presents video tapes on Eckankar every Sunday from 3 to 6 p.m. at 2037 13th St., Suite 13. Free. For information call 443-1610.

CHRISTIAN SINGLES OF BOULDER VALLEY meet for a coffee hour every Sunday at 7:30 p.m. at Shakey's Pizza, 1964 28th St. For information call 441-9515.

BRILLIG 'LIVE' will present classical guitar music by Terry Hunt at 8 p.m. Brillig Works Tearoom is at 1322 College Ave.

FIGURE 7–1   "What's Happening" from the *Colorado Daily*

3. What kind of workshop will William Burroughs lead this weekend?

_____

4. What number should you call to make reservations for watching the stars?

_____

5. Which radio station broadcasts the program *Ganges to the Nile?*

_____

6. Where will Terry Hunt play classical guitar on Sunday?

_____

7. How much does the seminar on "Adobe/Rammed Earth: Building with Earth" cost if you pay at the door?

_____

8. What's happening at 8:00 on Saturday morning?

_____

Exercise 7–14

Directions: *Scan the table of contents from* Newsweek *(a weekly news magazine) (Figure 7–2) to find the answers to the following questions. Write the answers in the spaces. Try to do this exercise as quickly as possible.*

1. What is the title of the "cover story," or "special report," of this issue of Newsweek?

_____

2. On what page can you read about Julio Iglesias, the singer?

_____

3. On what page can you read about the new IBM Personal Computer?

_____

4. What is the name of the new department that is introduced with this issue of *Newsweek?*

_____

5. On what page can you find the "Newsmakers" department?

_____

6. Who is the author of the book "Flashbacks"?

_____

TOP OF THE WEEK

Newsweek

JULY 11, 1983

Case of the Purloined Papers

The controversy over documents from Jimmy Carter's camp that were obtained by the Reagan staff during the 1980 presidential campaign heated up last week. White House staff members released a blizzard of Carter documents from their files, and the FBI began investigating just how the Reagan campaign got hold of the papers in the first place. **Page 20**

What the World Thinks of America

Loved, hated, misunderstood—and imitated—America remains the inescapable country. Its movies, pop music and especially TV have bypassed the traditional avenues of exchange between nations. A NEWSWEEK Poll shows that citizens of six countries, on three continents, believe U.S. influence abroad is on the rise. Another finding: foreigners perceive Americans as a good and productive people with an erratic or even dangerous government. **Page 44**

IBM Goes on the Offensive

Although it is less than two years old, IBM's Personal Computer has taken the market by storm. While independent firms race to devise new products for the PC, IBM's competitors are being outgunned. Yet small computers are only a part of IBM's drive to dominate markets in the information age. As the company applies its formidable research and marketing power to new technologies, AT&T and Japan Inc. face a serious challenge. **Page 56**

America's Olympic Hopefuls Gear Up for 1984

With this issue, NEWSWEEK introduces a new department, THE OLYMPICS, which will follow America's best athletes to the 1984 Summer and Winter games in Los Angeles and Sarajevo, Yugoslavia. This week's story reports on America's newfound confidence in its ability to compete internationally. The optimism is based on a bumper crop of U.S. hopefuls, including Carl Lewis (right) and Mary Decker, and on a more realistic approach to the big business of amateur sports. **Page 74**

CONTENTS

Cover: Photos by Jean-Louis Atlan—Sygma, Randy Taylor—Sygma, Greg Davis and James Andanson—Sygma. Inset photo by Bruce Hoertel.

Letters to the Editor should be sent to NEWSWEEK, 444 Madison Avenue, New York, N.Y. 10022, and subscription inquiries to NEWSWEEK, The NEWSWEEK Building, Livingston, N.J. 07039. NEWSWEEK (ISSN 0028-9604), July 11, 1983, Volume CII, No. 2, is published weekly, $39.00 a year, by NEWSWEEK, Inc., 10100 Santa Monica Boulevard, Los Angeles, Calif. 90067. Second Class postage paid at Los Angeles, Calif., and at additional mailing offices. POSTMASTERS: Send address changes to NEWSWEEK, The NEWSWEEK Building, Livingston, N.J. 07039.

FIGURE 7–2 Table of contents from *Newsweek* Copyright 1983 by Newsweek, Inc. *All rights reserved, reprinted by permission.*

7. In what department can you read about the chemical Dioxin?

_____

8. What is the name of the movie that is reviewed in this issue?

_____

The Denver Post Thursday, Aug. 18, 1983

TV AND CABLE LISTINGS

	CH 2 Independent	CH 4 NBC	CH 6 PBS	CH 7 CBS	CH 9 ABC	CH 31 Independent	CH 41 SIN	CH 57 RELIGIOUS
DAYTIME								
5 AM / 30	Sgt. Bilko / Religion	News, News at Sunrise		CBS Early News				...Can I Live? / Joy in the
6 AM / 30	Monkees / Blinky's Circus	News	6:15 Weather / Polka Dot Door	CBS Morning News	News	Jimmy Swaggart / Jimmy Swaggart	Jimmy Swaggart	Morning / The Answer
7 AM / 30	Bugs Bunny / Popeye/Woody	Today	Powerhouse / Mister Rogers	Powerhouse	Good Morning America	Spiderman / Superheroes	El Chapulin / Eduardo II	Lester Sumrall / The LaHayes
8 AM / 30	Flintstones / Fun Club	"	Program/Gifted / Reading Rainbow	$25,000 Pyra. / Child's Play	"	Groovie Goolies / Spacecoaster	El Nino	AIA Sports / Joy in the
9 AM / 30	Bonanza / "	Donahue	Biology / English Grammar	The Price Is Right	Richard Hogue / Loving	700 Club	Pasiones Encendidas	Morning / Get in Shape
10 AM / 30	Rockford Files	Little House on the Prairie	World History II / Amer. History II	Jokers Wild / Tic Tac Dough	Family Feud / Ryan's Hope	Merv Griffin	Hoy Mismo	Praise the Lord / "
11 AM / 30	Soar/Eagles / INN News	Dream House / Diff'rent Strokes	Sesame Street / "	The Young and the Restless	All My Children	20 Minute Wkt.	"	Praise the Lord / "
12 PM / 30	I Love Lucy / Dick Van Dyke	News / Wheel Fortune	Polka Dot Door / Mister Rogers	News / As the World	News / Rhoda	Medical Center	Mundo Latino	Behind Scenes / Jimmy Swaggart
1 PM / 30	Real McCoys / Andy Griffith	Another World	Great Performances	Turns / Capitol	General Hospital	MOVIE: / 'Tiger's Claw'	En San Antonio / Vivir Enamorada	Sermons/Science / Kenneth Hagin
2 PM / 30	Beverly Hillbillies / Pink Panther	Days of Our Lives	Bonaventure / Food, Wine...	Guiding Light	One Life to Live	"	Senorita Andrea	This Is the Life / ...Can I Live?
3 PM / 30	Tom & Jerry / Scooby Doo	Sale of Century / Little House on	Lilias/Yoga/You / Sesame Street	People's Court / Wonder Woman	Three's Company / Muppet Show	Popeye & Friends	Quiero Gritar / Tu Nombre	Heritage Singers / Lester Sumrall
4 PM / 30	Superfriends / Leave It Beaver	the Prairie / News	Biology	Barney Miller	Hour Magazine / —	Heckle & Jeckle / Superheroes	Dejame Vivir	Praise the Lord / "
5 PM / 30	What Happening / Carter Country	News / "	English Grammar / World History II	News / "	News / "	Buck Rogers	Reporter 41 / Noticiero	Praise the Lord / "
EVENING								
6 PM / 30	Bob Newhart / Sanford & Son	NBC News / P.M. Magazine	Amer. History II / Business Report	CBS News / Entertain Tonight	ABC News / Sundown	B.J./Lobo	Soledad / Chiquilladas	Behind Scenes / Bible Bowl
7 PM / 30	For the Love / of a Child	Gimme a Break / Mama's Family	MacNeil/Lehrer / Wine/Pleasure!	NFL Exhi- / bition	On Hollywood / Too Close...	Hawaii Five-O	No Empujen / Noche de	Lordship/Christ / Roger McDuff
8 PM / 30	Going / Platinum	National Snoop / Cheers	Sneak Previews / Sea Power	Football: / New York	Reggie / It Takes Two	Mannix	Gala / Gabriel/Gabriela	Dwight Thompson
9 PM / 30	News / INN News	Hill Street Blues / "	Meeting of / the Minds	at / Cincinnati	20/20	Kojak	24 Horas	Praise the Lord / "
10 PM / 30	Benny Hill / Mary Hartman	News / The Best	No, Honestly / Sports America	News / Magnum P.I.	News / M*A*S*H	Odd Couple / Twilight Zone	CINE: / 'La Morocha'	Praise the Lord / "
11 PM / 30	Saturday Night / "	of Carson / Star Trek	Last Chance	Quincy	ABC Nightline	Twilight Zone / MOVIE:	"	Praise the Lord / "
12 AM / 30	It Takes / a Thief	" / David		12:50 Detector	Tom Cottle / Hit City	The Flying / Missile'		Behind Scenes / Shockwaves
1 AM / 30	MOVIE: / 'Run for Cover'	Letterman / News		1:20 CBS / Nightwatch	Sundown / News	"		Praise the Lord / "
2 AM / 30	" / "	2:10 MOVIE: / 'Melody'		(JJP)	2:10 Colorado / 2:40 CNN News			Praise the Lord / "
3 AM / 30	News / MOVIE:	"		CBS News / Nightwatch	"			Praise the Lord / "
4 AM / 30	Trigger Jr.'	" / NBC News		Cont.				Behind Scenes / Best Day of Life

FIGURE 7-3 "TV and Cable Listings" from _The Denver Post_

Exercise 7-15

Directions: *Scan the "TV and Cable Listings" from* The Denver Post *(Figure 7-3) to find the answers to the following questions. Write your answers in the spaces. Try to do this exercise as quickly as possible.*

1. What program is on Channel 7 (CH 7) at 5:00 A.M.?

   _____

2. What program is on Channel 9 (CH 9) at 7:30 A.M.?

   _____

3. At what time does the "Today" show begin on Channel 4?

   _____

4. On what channel can you watch the "McNeil/Lehrer Report"?

   _____

5. The network news programs (NBC News, CBS News, and ABC News) are all broadcast at the same time. At what time can you watch these programs?

   _____

6. The "Sesame Street" program is broadcast at two different times. What are these two times?

   _____ and _____

7. On what channel can you watch the Spanish language program "Mundo Latino"?

   _____

8. At what time can you watch the ABC news magazine program "20/20"?

   _____

   On what channel can you watch this program?

   _____

UNIT 8 Reading Passages

WHAT'S NEW

FROM YOUR VALENTINE

HEREDITY OR ENVIRONMENT

What's New

Questions for Discussion

Directions: *Before you begin this chapter, try to answer these questions about the topic of the chapter. Discuss your answers with other students in your class.*

1. How do you usually find out about the news?
   a. by reading a newspaper or news magazine
   b. by listening to the radio
   c. by watching television
   d. by talking to friends
   e. in all of these ways

2. What type of news are you most interested in?
   a. international news
   b. news about your country
   c. news about your field of study
   d. sports news

   e. other news (please specify): _____

3. What is the name of your favorite newspaper or magazine?

   _____

4. Do you think it is important to find out about the news every day? Why or why not?

   _____

5. Do you think talking about the news is a good way to practice English? Why or why not?

_____

Voacbulary Preparation

Directions: *Read the following paragraphs and use context clues to guess the meanings of the underlined words. Then write a definition for each underlined word in the space. The first one is done for you.*

Our newspaper publishes two editions: a national edition and an international edition. The national edition is published in New York and is distributed in every state in the United States. The international edition is published in Paris and distributed in most of the countries of Europe, Africa, Asia, and Latin America.

1. **published** = _printed_____

2. **distributed** = _____

Each television station broadcasts on a different channel. These channels are numbered (for example, channel 4, channel 7, channel 9). Most American cities have at least four television stations, and each station sends out programs on its own channel. In addition, most of these cities also have special cable television stations. Cable stations send out their programs on special wires, unlike other television stations which broadcast their programs through the air.

3. **broadcast** = _____

4. **cable television** = _____

Newspapers are divided into different sections for different kinds of news. The first part of the newspaper is devoted to the most important news of the day. Then there are sections for local, national, and international news. The editorial section is next, with news analysis, opinions, and political cartoons. Most newspapers contain a business section, a sports section, and a section for classified advertisements. Some newspapers have a features section, which is devoted to special articles about interesting events and ideas. Sometimes newspapers publish additional sections, or supplements, such as advertising supplements describing goods for sale at local stores.

5. **sections** = _____

6. **features** = _____

7. **supplements** = _____

8. **advertising** = _____

Text

What's New

In the modern world, it is important to be well-informed. Success in many fields depends on getting the latest information. To keep up with what is happening in the world, well-informed people read newspapers and news magazines. They listen to the news on the radio and they watch it on television. Owners of home computers can even receive their news directly from the wire services—news agencies that supply newspapers, magazines, radio, and television with news reports—through special telephone links.

Most people read newspapers for the news of the day. The typical daily newspaper contains articles about local, regional, national, and international news, as well as sports news, weather reports, editorials, and other features. In large cities, newspaper readers can often choose between a "morning paper" distributed early in the morning and an "evening paper" distributed at the end of the workday. Most American newspapers also publish an enlarged Sunday edition containing articles about the news of the day and of the week, plus a number of entertainment and advertising supplements. Daily newspapers are designed to be read quickly by busy people looking for specific information. The Sunday papers, on the other hand, are intended to entertain as well as inform, and they tend to be read leisurely by all members of the family. Other types of newspapers include campus newspapers, written by students at universities, and weekly newspapers, usually intended for a specific audience.

News magazines such as *Time, Newsweek,* and *U.S. News and World Report* are published weekly. They contain articles about the important national and international news of the week, and special sections are devoted to news about such areas as business, science, education, and the arts. News magazines are a popular source of general information on a wide range of recent events. They also feature longer articles dealing with the influence of current events on modern life.

Radio and television present the important news of the hour. Many radio stations in the U.S. broadcast news every hour, and a few all-news stations broadcast news and news commentary programs all day. Most commercial television stations have news programs in the evening (beginning at 5:00 or 6:00 P.M.) and at night (beginning at 10:00 or 11:00 P.M.). The evening news generally consists of a national network news program and a local news program, while at night it is usually a local program. In addition, some TV stations offer early morning news, late night news, and weekly "news magazine" programs. Cable television networks in some cities offer foreign language news and all-news channels.

Students learning English in English-speaking countries find the news a useful source of language practice. To improve their listening comprehension, they listen to the news on the radio and watch it on television. Then they check their comprehension by reading newspapers and news magazines. Everyone likes to talk about the news. In the office, on the campus, at parties, or on the street, conversations often begin with questions like "What's new?", "What's happening?", or "Have you heard about . . . ?" By staying well informed, these students find it easier to enter into conversations about the news.

Comprehension Questions

Directions: *True or false? Write "T" in the space if the statement is* true. *Write "F" if it is* false.

_____ 1. Newspapers, magazines, radio, and television get news reports from the wire services.

_____ 2. Newspapers contain the news of the day.

_____ 3. Sunday newspapers are designed to be read quickly by busy people looking for specific information.

_____ 4. Campus newspapers and weekly newspapers are written by university students.

_____ 5. News magazines are usually published weekly.

_____ 6. People listen to radio and television for the important news of the hour.

_____ 7. On commercial television stations, the evening news program is usually a local program while at night it is a national network program.

_____ 8. Some radio and television stations broadcast news all day.

_____ 9. Most American television stations offer foreign language news programs.

_____ 10. Students learning English listen to the news on the radio and watch it on television to improve their reading comprehension.

Directions: *Circle the letter of the* best *answer.*

1. Which type of newspaper is distributed at the end of the workday?
   a. a morning paper
   b. an evening paper
   c. a campus newspaper
   d. a Sunday newspaper

2. Which type of newspaper contains a number of entertainment and advertising supplements?
   a. a morning paper
   b. an evening paper
   c. a campus newspaper
   d. a Sunday newspaper

3. Longer articles dealing with the influence of current events on modern life are often found in _____.
   a. daily newspapers
   b. Sunday newspapers
   c. news magazines
   d. network news programs

4. Weekly news magazines are intended for a _____ audience.
   a. general
   b. specific
   c. university
   d. family

5. News bulletins are broadcast every hour on many _____.
   a. commercial television stations
   b. cable television networks
   c. radio stations
   d. "news magazine" programs

6. Special telephone links make it possible for owners of home computers to receive news from _____.
   a. newspapers
   b. magazines

  c. wire services

  d. radio and television stations

Directions: *What's the difference? Find the answers to the following questions in the text and write them in the spaces.*

1. What is the difference between a "morning paper" and an "evening paper"?

  _____

  _____

2. What is the difference between a daily newspaper and a Sunday newspaper?

  _____

  _____

3. Most commercial television stations broadcast news programs in the evening and at night. What is the difference between an evening news program and a night news program?

  _____

  _____

  Outlining

Directions: *Complete the following outline of the first three paragraphs of the text. (See Unit 7 Paragraph Study for an explanation of* outline.*) The first line is done for you.*

 I. *In the modern world, it is important to be well-informed.*

  A. Success in many fields depends on it.

  B. Read _____ and _____

  C. Listen to _____

  D. Watch _____

  E. Owners of home computers can get news from wire services.

 II. _____

  A. Daily newspapers contain

   1. _____

   2. _____

B. Sunday newspapers contain

   1. _____

   2. _____

C. Daily newspapers are designed to _____

_____

D. Sunday newspapers are intended to _____

_____

E. Other types of newspapers

   1. _____

   2. _____

III. _____

A. Articles about _____

B. Special sections about _____

C. _____

D. Longer articles about _____

_____

Additional Reading

The Commercial and Public Networks

Most radio and television stations in the United States are commercial stations; that is, they get their money from advertisements or commercials. Private companies buy radio and television time from the commercial stations in order to advertise their products. Cable television stations are also commercial stations, although they do not usually have advertisements. In order to watch cable stations, people must pay the cable TV company a certain amount of money each month.

Public radio and television stations, on the other hand, do not have advertisements and people do not have to pay to watch them. These stations get their money from the government, from private companies, and from some of the people who watch or listen to their programs. The Federal government and some large corporations give grants, large gifts of money, to the public stations. Small businesses and individual people also donate money to support their local public radio and television stations.

ABC, CBS, and NBC are the three major commercial radio and television networks in the United States. Most local commercial radio and TV stations get their programs from one of these national networks. For example, each network has a TV news program in the evening, which the local stations broadcast in addition to their own local news programs.

Public radio and television stations also get programs from national networks. The National Public Radio network provides programs for local public radio stations. "Morning Edition" and "All Things Considered" are two news programs that NPR provides. The Public Broadcasting Service and National Educational Television networks provide programs for local public television stations. PBS provides news programs like the "MacNeil/Lehrer Newshour" as well as cultural programs. NET provides educational programs for schools as well as programs like "Sesame Street" for preschool children.

Vocabulary in Context

Directions: *Find definitions for the following words in the text. The first one is done for you.*

1. **commercials** = *advertisements* _____

2. **grants** = _____

3. **donate** = _____

Initials: Initials are the first letters of a name. For example, the initials ABC stand for the American Broadcasting Company, the initials CBS stand for the Columbia Broadcasting System, and the initials NBC stand for the National Broadcasting Company.

1. What do the initials NPR stand for?

_____

2. What do the initials PBS stand for?

_____

3. What do the initials NET stand for?

_____

Sentence Completion

Directions: *Use information from the text to complete the following sentences.*

1. Most commercial radio and television stations get their money from

_____

2. Cable television stations get their money from

_____

3. Public radio and television stations get their money from

   (1) _____

   (2) _____

   (3) _____

4. Both commercial and public stations get their programs from

_____

The Wire Services

Most newspaper, radio, and television news comes from special news agencies called "wire services." They are called "wire" services because they send and receive many of their news reports over telephone and telegraph wires, although most wire services today use radio, communication satellites, and computer links as well. Of the four major wire services in the world today two are based in the United States, one in Britain, and one in the Soviet Union.

The Associated Press (AP) is a non-profit membership association and its headquarters are in New York City's Rockefeller Plaza. AP began in 1848 as an unofficial newsgathering cooperative for New York newspapers. Today 10,000 newspapers, radio stations, and television stations in more than 100 countries receive news reports and photographs from AP. 1300 of these newspapers and 3600 of the radio and television stations are in the United States. AP is known as a conservative wire service: most of its stories agree with the opinions of the rich families who own many of its member newspapers, and its foreign news often follows official U.S. government policy.

In 1958, the United Press and the International News Service joined together to form UPI, the United Press International. UPI is a privately-owned business with its headquarters on New York's 42nd Street. It serves 6972 newspapers, radio stations, and television stations all over the world, including 1131 newspapers and 3650 radio and television stations in the U.S. UPI uses a modern computerized system with video typewriters and computer links between offices to send and receive news reports quickly. However, UPI's news reports are often not very interesting and they contain little analysis or opinion. As a result, many people think that at UPI speed is more important than good news reporting.

Paul Julius Reuter was a German expatriate who started a financial news service for banks in London in 1858. Later he extended the service to newspapers, and then he included general news with financial news. Today, the Reuters news agency has over 3000 subscribers in 155 countries, many of them

Third World countries. It is well known as a source of accurate and objective news reports on international events. Reuters is a non-profit organization and its headquarters are located in Fleet Street, the newspaper district of London.

TASS is the major news agency of the Soviet Union. It began as ROSTA in 1918 and became TASS in 1925. In 1970 it became an independent self-sustaining news agency, but it remains under the control of the Soviet Political Bureau. 6000 subscribers receive news reports from TASS headquarters in Moscow. Most of these subscribers are in the Soviet Union, but many are in Third World countries. For TASS, the political results of news reports are more important than speed, so all news reports are carefully prepared before they are sent out and they generally sound like official government statements.

Organizing Information

Directions: *Use information from the passage to complete the following table about the four major wire services. Some of the information is given, but some is missing.*

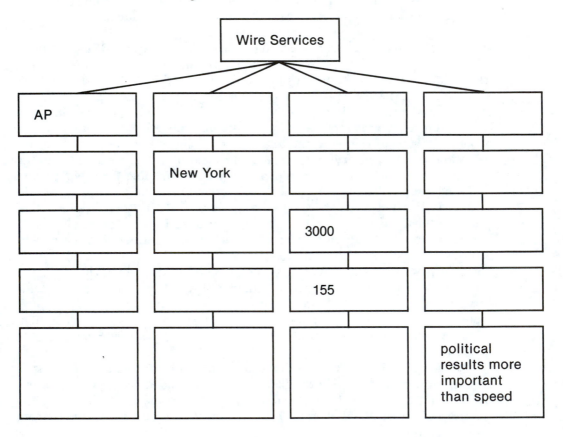

Similarities and Differences

Directions: *Write answers to the following questions. The information in the preceding table will help you, but you will also need to look for information in the passage.*

1. What is the *one main difference* between UPI and TASS?

   _____

   _____

2. What is the *one main similarity* between AP and Reuters?

   _____

   _____

3. Which wire service has the largest number of subscribers?

   _____

   How many subscribers does it have?

   _____

4. Which wire service serves the largest number of countries?

   _____

   How many countries does it serve?

   _____

Directions: *What do you think? Write answers to the following questions and discuss your answers with other students in your class.*

1. Which wire service do you think is the best source of international news? Why?

   _____

   _____

2. Which wire service does the *author* think is the best? Why?

   _____

   _____

3. Most wire services work like businesses: they buy and sell news. Do you think this is a good way to distribute the news? Why or why not?

   _____

   _____

4. The four major wire services are based in developed countries (the U.S., the U.K., and the USSR) but many of their subscribers are in developing countries in the Third World. As a result, some Third World countries are trying to start a wire service for Third World news. Do you think a wire service for Third World countries is necessary? Why or why not?

_____

_____

From Your Valentine

Questions for Discussion

Directions: *Before you begin this chapter, try to answer these questions about the topic of the chapter. Discuss your answers with other students in your class.*

1. Does your country have any unusual holidays? Try to describe one of them.

_____

_____

2. Americans exchange greeting cards, such as birthday cards and Christmas cards, on a variety of occasions. When do people in your country send greeting cards to each other?

_____

_____

3. How many of the following holidays do you know about? Put a check (✔) beside the ones you know.

Thanksgiving _____   Groundhog Day _____

Cinco de Mayo _____   April Fool's Day _____

Chanukah _____   Sadie Hawkins Day _____

Halloween _____   St. Valentine's Day _____

Vocabulary Preparation

The following illustrations will help you understand some of the vocabulary in the text.

FIGURE 8–1 Vocabulary for "From Your Valentine"

Directions: *Read the following sentences and use context clues to guess the meanings of the underlined words. Then write a definition for each word in the space. The first one is done for you.*

1. Greeting cards always have <u>messages printed</u> on them. For example, the message "Happy Birthday" is printed on birthday cards, and "Merry Christmas" is the message usually printed on Christmas cards.

   message = *words that give information* _____

   printed = _____

2. The policeman began to <u>chase</u> the thief when he saw him take the money, but he could not <u>catch</u> him because the thief was a very fast runner.

   chase = _____

   catch = _____

3. Jeanie is the funniest person I know. She can always make me laugh when she tells a <u>joke</u>, and she often plays <u>tricks</u> on me. Yesterday, for example, we were eating at a restaurant when she shouted, "Look behind you! The President just came into the room!" When I turned to look, she took the last piece of cake from my plate. Of course, the President was not there; she had <u>tricked</u> me in order to get my last piece of cake.

   joke = _____

   trick = _____

4. The people of my village have an interesting <u>legend</u> about the <u>origin</u> of clouds. According to the story, clouds are really puffs of smoke coming from the fires of the sun.

   legend = _____

   origin = _____

5. Americans <u>celebrate</u> Labor Day on the first Monday in September. On this day, all workers <u>are supposed to</u> have a holiday.

   celebrate = _____

   are supposed to = _____

Text

From Your Valentine

   Considering the number of ethnic groups that make up the U.S. population, it is not surprising that Americans have a variety of different holidays. From Thanksgiving to Cinco de Mayo, from Chanukah to the Chinese New

Year, they are seldom at a loss for a reason to celebrate. Some of these holidays are rather unusual. Some examples follow.

Groundhog Day, February 2:

The groundhog, a small burrowing animal also known as a woodchuck, is supposed to come out of his hole to look for his shadow on this day. As the legend goes, if he fails to see his shadow it means spring has come; if he sees it he returns to his hole to sleep, for winter will continue for another six weeks.

April Fool's Day, April 1:

Don't believe anything you hear on this day of tricks and jokes designed to make you an "April Fool"!

Halloween, October 31:

After dark, children dressed like ghosts and witches go from house to house shouting "Trick or treat!" The people they visit must fill their bags with candy and other treats or else the children will play tricks on them.

Sadie Hawkins Day, the first Saturday after November 11:

Traditionally, it is the boys who chase the girls, but on Sadie Hawkins Day a girl can keep any boy she can catch.

On February 14 Americans celebrate another unusual holiday, St. Valentine's Day, a special day for lovers. Valentines are cards—usually red and shaped like hearts—with messages of love written on them. Lovers send these cards to each other, often anonymously, on St. Valentine's Day.

The origins of this holiday are uncertain, but according to one legend, it gets its name from a Christian priest named Valentine who lived in Rome during the third century after Christ. His job was to perform marriages for Christian couples. Unfortunately, the Emperor of Rome, Claudius II, did not allow Christian marriages, so they had to be performed in secret. Eventually Valentine was arrested and put into prison. While in prison he fell in love with the daughter of the prison guard.

After one year, the Emperor offered to release Valentine if he would agree to stop performing these secret marriages. Valentine refused, so the Emperor sentenced him to death. Valentine was executed in 270 A.D. on February 14, the same day the Romans worshiped their goddess of marriage, Juno. Before he was killed, Valentine sent a love letter to the daughter of the prison guard. He signed the letter "from your Valentine." That was the first valentine.

The next valentine was sent in 1415 A.D. Charles, Duke of Orleans sent the valentine to his wife while he was a prisoner in the Tower of London. His valentine is now on exhibit in the British Museum. The first commercially printed valentines did not appear until 1809. Some of these valentines were not messages of love. Comic valentines, or "penny dreadfuls" as they were called, were often funny and sometimes insulting. The "Golden Age" of valentines began in the 1840s when valentine makers started making elaborate and expensive valentines.

Jonathan King became famous as a publisher of beautiful and unusual valentines in Britain in the 1870s. Esther Howland was the first to publish valentines in the United States, in the 1860s. She created handmade designs for valentines, which cost as much as thirty-five dollars.

Today, millions of Americans send and receive valentines on St. Valentine's Day. Whether it is an expensive heart-shaped box of chocolates from a secret admirer or a simple handmade card from a child, a valentine is a very special message of love.

Comprehension Questions

Directions: *True or false? Write "T" if the statement is true; write "F" if it is false.*

_____ 1. Americans have a variety of different holidays.

_____ 2. On Groundhog Day, people play tricks on each other.

_____ 3. Halloween is a children's holiday.

_____ 4. On Sadie Hawkins Day, the boys chase the girls.

_____ 5. St. Valentine's Day is a special day for lovers.

_____ 6. The first valentine was sent by Charles, Duke of Orleans.

_____ 7. St. Valentine performed marriages for the Emperor.

_____ 8. The first person to publish valentines in the U.S. was Esther Howland.

_____ 9. Many Americans send cards to each other on St. Valentine's Day.

_____ 10. A valentine is an expensive heart-shaped box of chocolates.

Directions: *Circle the letter of the best answer.*

1. Americans have a variety of holidays because of _____.

   a. the large population of the U.S.
   b. the number of ethnic groups in the U.S.
   c. the unusual nature of these holidays
   d. the loss of a reason to celebrate

2. The first valentine was sent to _____.
   a. Claudius II, Emperor of Rome
   b. the wife of Charles, Duke of Orleans
   c. the goddess of marriage
   d. the daughter of a prison guard

3. The "Golden Age" of valentines began when _____.
   a. elaborate and expensive valentines were made
   b. the first commercially printed valentines appeared
   c. comic valentines were first printed
   d. Americans started sending valentines to each other

4. Today, people send valentines to each other in order to
   _____.
   a. perform marriages
   b. fall in love
   c. show their love
   d. insult each other

5. The legend of St. Valentine is _____.
   a. one of the possible origins of this holiday
   b. a true story from Roman history
   c. the certain origin of St. Valentine's Day
   d. one of the unusual American legends

Directions: *Find answers to the following questions in the text. Write the answers in the spaces.*

1. Why are Americans seldom at a loss for a reason to celebrate?

   _____

   _____

2. What kind of holiday is St. Valentine's Day?

   _____

   _____

3. What do people do on St. Valentine's Day?

   _____

   _____

4. What is a valentine?

_____

_____

5. According to legend, who was St. Valentine?

_____

_____

6. Why was St. Valentine executed?

_____

_____

Outlining

Directions: *Complete the following outline of the Valentine legend by finding the appropriate information in the text and writing it in the spaces.*

I. St. Valentine's Day gets its name from _____

_____

   A. Lived in _____ during _____

   B. Job: _____

      1. Emperor did not allow _____

      2. therefore Valentine was _____

   C. While _____

_____

II. The first _____

   A. Emperor offered to release Valentine if _____

_____

   B. Valentine _____, so _____

_____

      1. executed on _____

      2. same day _____

   C. Before he was killed _____

_____

      1. signed _____

      2. this letter was _____

Directions: *What do you think? Answer these questions and discuss your answers with other students in your class.*

1. Is it important to know about unusual holidays like St. Valentine's Day, Groundhog Day, April Fool's Day, Halloween, and Sadie Hawkins Day? Why or why not?

2. According to legend, St. Valentine was executed on the same day the Romans worshiped Juno. Why do you think Emperor Claudius II chose this day for Valentine's execution?

3. Are all valentines expensive today? Why or why not?

4. Are valentines only sent by lovers? Why or why not?

5. Compare St. Valentine's Day with Thanksgiving and Cinco de Mayo (see Unit 7 Paragraph Study Exercise 7–11). How are these holidays similar? How are they different?

6. Valentine lived in Rome during the third century after Christ, and he was executed in 270 A.D. What do you think "A.D." means? What years are included in the "third century after Christ"?

Heredity or Environment

Photo by Joan Ramsay

Discussion Questions

Before you begin this chapter, try to answer the following questions about the topic of the chapter. Then discuss your answers with other students in your class.

1. Two children who are born together are called twins. Do you know any twins? If you do, in what ways are they similar? In what ways are they different?

2. Every child knows how to eat and drink. However, small children must learn how to use a spoon or a cup. Eating and drinking are *instincts*—they do not have to be learned—but using a spoon or a cup is *learned* behavior. What are some more examples of instincts and learned behavior?

3. When a family goes to live in a different country, it is often difficult for the parents to speak a different language, eat different kinds of food, and understand the ideas of the people in the new country. The children, however, often find it easier to live in the new country. Why is it easier for the children?

Vocabulary Preparation

Directions: *Read the following paragraph and use context clues to guess the meanings of the underlined words. Then answer the questions.*

John and Marsha are married, but they have different religions. John is a Christian; he goes to a Catholic church on Sundays. Marsha is Jewish; she goes to a synagogue on Saturdays. John and Marsha met on a kibbutz in Israel where they were both working in the fields with young people from many different countries, growing vegetables and other crops. When they returned to the United States, John and Marsha got married. John got a job in an appliance store selling electric can-openers, toasters, washing machines, and dishwashers, and Marsha became a teacher. They both work very hard for nine months every year. In the summer they take a three-month vacation and go to Israel in order to visit their friends from the kibbutz where they first met.

1. A Catholic church is _____.

   a. a Jewish place of worship

   b. a Christian place of worship

   c. a place in Israel

   d. a place in the United States

2. A <u>synagogue</u> is _____.

   a. a Jewish place of worship

   b. a Christian place of worship

   c. a place in Israel

   d. a place in the United States

3. A <u>kibbutz</u> is a type of _____.

   a. holiday camp

   b. international meeting

   c. town in Israel

   d. farm in Israel

4. An <u>appliance</u> is a(n) _____.

   a. job in a store

   b. machine to make work easier

   c. electric can-opener

   d. teaching job

5. When people take a <u>vacation</u>, they _____.

   a. work very hard at their jobs

   b. leave their jobs completely

   c. stop working for a short time

   d. leave their countries

Directions: *Read the following sentences and use context clues to guess the meanings of the underlined words. Then write a definition for each word in the space. The first one is done for you.*

It is easy to observe people's <u>behavior</u>—we only need to watch what they do. It is much more difficult to observe their <u>thoughts</u> because we cannot look inside their brains to see what they are thinking. Besides, people can hide their thoughts easily when they do not want others to know what they think.

1. **behavior:** *what people do*

2. **thoughts:** _____

When we <u>compare</u> the <u>height</u> and <u>weight</u> of children who like to drink milk with the height and weight of children who refuse to drink milk, we find that children who drink milk are larger than those who do not. On the average, children who drink milk are 4 inches (10 cm.) taller and 12 pounds (5 kg.) heavier than children who do not drink milk.

3. **compare:** _____

4. **height:** _____

5. **weight:** _____

In most families, small children are brought up by their mother and father. In some places, small children are brought up by grandparents or aunts and uncles, and in a few places the whole community is responsible for bringing up the children. When one parent dies or when the parents are divorced, small children may be brought up by only one parent.

4. **brought up:** _____

The size of a person's feet is usually determined by the person's height. For example, a tall person (6½ feet or 2 m. tall) will probably have large feet, but a short person (4½ feet or 1.5m. tall) will probably have small feet. This is because a tall person needs larger feet to support his or her body than a short person.

7. **determined:** _____

Text

Heredity or Environment

Oscar grew up in Czechoslovakia during World War II. His grandmother brought him up to be a good Catholic, and in school he learned to be a good Nazi. He was taught to shout "Heil Hitler!" and to hate Jews and other enemies of the Third Reich. He wanted to join the Hitler Youth Corps of the Nazi army, but the war ended before he could. Now he is a supervisor in a factory in Germany; he belongs to a trade union, takes vacations in Italy and Yugoslavia, and skis in the Alps. He believes in strict discipline and expects his wife to do whatever he tells her to do without asking questions.

Jack grew up in Trinidad, an island in the Carribean Sea. As a boy he went to the synagogue, studied Hebrew, and learned to be a good Jew. He hated Nazis and cheered when the British beat the Germans in the war movies he loved to watch. When he was seventeen years old, he went to Israel to work on a kibbutz. Now he owns a clothing and appliance store in California. He works long hours and seldom takes a vacation. His political ideas are somewhat liberal and he accepts the feminist movement.

Oscar and Jack are identical twins, separated when they were babies by their parents' divorce. Jack was brought up by their Jewish father in Trinidad, but his brother Oscar went to live with their mother's family in Czechoslovakia. In fact, Oscar did not know he was Jewish until Jack found him in Germany in 1954. Jack is proud to be a Jew, but Oscar still does not like to talk about his Jewish heritage. Yet the twins are similar in many ways. They both like spicy food and sweet drinks. In school they both did well in sports but poorly in mathematics. They share some of the same idiosyncracies as well, such as flushing the toilet before and after using it.

Are thoughts and behavior determined by heredity (the genetic characteristics children inherit from their parents) or by environment (the influences children receive from the world around them)? Social scientists have long been interested in this question; the results of "twin studies" are particularly interesting to them. Twin studies are studies of the similarities and differences between twins. There are two types of twins: *identical* twins, who look exactly the same because they have identical genetic characteristics, and *fraternal* twins, who have different genetic characteristics. In a 1937 study, Newman, Freeman, and Halzinger found that identical twins are more similar in height and weight than fraternal twins. Because identical twins have the same genetic characteristics, the conclusion was that size is determined more by heredity than by environment. In 1962, James Shields compared the height, weight, and intelligence of identical twins who were brought up together (in the same environment) with those of identical twins brought up apart (in different environments). He found that, although the differences were small, identical twins who were brought up together were more similar than those brought up apart. Shields concluded that height, weight, and intelligence are largely determined by heredity. However, because of the differences between identical twins brought up together and those brought up apart, these characteristics may be partly determined by environment.

In the case of Oscar and Jack, heredity seems to determine physical and mental abilities, tastes, and idiosyncratic behavior. Environment seems to determine thought. However, these findings are far from conclusive. We cannot draw conclusions from these results alone; more twins must be studied and the results carefully considered before any real conclusions can be drawn. Furthermore, some scientists question the results of twin studies because many of the environmental factors are difficult to control. For example, twins who are brought up apart are often brought up by members of the same family, so their environments may be quite similar. Consequently, no answer has yet been found to the "heredity or environment" question.

Comprehension Questions

Directions: *True or false? Write "T" in the space if the statement is* true. *Write "F" if it is* false.

_____ 1. Oscar was brought up by his grandmother.

_____ 2. Jack grew up on an island in the Carribean Sea.

_____ 3. Oscar and Jack have similar jobs today.

_____ 4. Oscar is proud to be a Jew.

_____ 5. Jack did well in school but Oscar did poorly.

_____ 6. Both Oscar and Jack flush the toilet before and after using it.

_____ 7. "Twin studies" are studies of the similarities and differences between identical twins.

_____ 8. Twin studies show that height, weight, and intelligence are determined by both heredity and environment.

_____ 9. From the case of Oscar and Jack, we can conclude that thought is determined by environment.

_____ 10. Scientists agree that an answer to the "heredity or environment" question can be found only by conducting more twin studies.

Directions: *Circle the letter of the* best *answer.*

1. After their parents' divorce, Oscar and Jack _____.
   a. went to live with their mother's family
   b. were brought up by their father
   c. never saw each other again
   d. were separated until 1954

2. Although Oscar and Jack are similar in many ways, they seem to be different in _____.
   a. physical ability
   b. mental ability
   c. idiosyncratic behavior
   d. thought

3. Identical twins are more similar than fraternal twins because

   _____.

   a. they have the same mother
   b. they have the same genetic characteristics
   c. they were brought up together
   d. they were born at the same time

4. The conclusion of Newman, Freeman, and Halzinger's 1937 twin study was that _____.

   a. identical twins are more similar than fraternal twins

   b. identical twins are taller and heavier than fraternal twins

   c. size is determined by height, weight, and environment

   d. size is determined more by heredity than by environment

5. Shields (1962) drew a slightly different conclusion from his study because _____.

   a. he also compared the intelligence of the twins in his study

   b. he compared twins brought up together with those brought up apart

   c. only identical twins were included in his study

   d. all of the environmental factors were carefully controlled

6. No answer has yet been found to the "heredity or environment" question because _____.

   a. most environments are quite similar

   b. the results of twin studies are not considered conclusive

   c. twins are often brought up by members of the same family

   d. it is difficult to control heredity factors

Similarities and Differences

Directions: *Use information from the text to complete the following tables about the similarities and differences between Oscar and Jack.*

DIFFERENCES

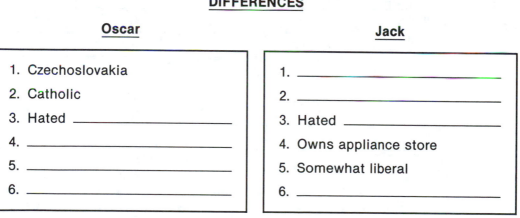

Oscar	Jack
1. Czechoslovakia	1. _____
2. Catholic	2. _____
3. Hated _____	3. Hated _____
4. _____	4. Owns appliance store
5. _____	5. Somewhat liberal
6. _____	6. _____

SIMILARITIES

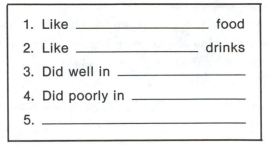

1. Like _____ food
2. Like _____ drinks
3. Did well in _____
4. Did poorly in _____
5. _____

Outlining

Directions: *Complete the following outline of paragraphs 4 and 5 in the text.*

I. _____

_____

  A. Twin studies: _____

     1. _____

       a. _____

_____

       b. _____

_____

     2. _____

       a. _____

_____

       b. _____

  B. Oscar and Jack

     1. _____

_____

     2. _____

  C. Cannot draw conclusions

     1. _____

     2. _____

a. _____

b. _____

D. _____

Guided Summary

Directions: *Write the answers to the following questions about the main ideas of the text. Your answers will form a summary of the text.*

1. What is the "heredity or environment" question?

   _____

   _____

2. What do twin studies show about the differences between fraternal and identical twins?

   _____

   _____

3. What does Shields' study show about the differences between identical twins brought up together and those brought up apart?

   _____

   _____

4. How are the conclusions of Shields' study different from those of the 1937 study?

   _____

   _____

5. Which characteristics seem to be determined by heredity?

   _____

   _____

6. Which characteristics seem to be determined by environment?

   _____

   _____

7. Why are the results of twin studies "far from conclusive"?

   _____

   _____

8. What is the answer to the "heredity or environment" question?

_____

_____

Directions: *What do you think? Write answers to the following questions and discuss your answers with other students in your class.*

1. Do you think scientists will find an answer to the "heredity or environment" question in the future? Why or why not?

2. Twin studies are one source of information about the "heredity or environment" question, but some scientists question the results of these studies. Can you think of ways to improve twin studies so that better results can be obtained?

3. People from the same country often have similar thoughts and behavior. Is this determined by heredity or environment? Give reasons to support your answer.